FORMULA 1
DRIVERS

The Stories of the Hottest Drivers & the Great Legendary Racers

Glenda J. Fordham

OVER
TIME
BOOKS

The Publisher: OverTime Books is an imprint of Éditions de la Montagne Verte

Library and Archives Canada Cataloguing in Publication

Fordham, Glenda J., 1953–

     Formula one drivers: the stories of the hottest drivers and the great legendary racers/ Glenda J. Fordham.

Includes bibliographical references.

ISBN 10: 1-897277-13-X

ISBN 13: 978-1-897277-13-3

     1. Grand Prix racing—Biography. 2. Grand Prix racing—History. 3. Automobile racing drivers—Biography. I. Title.

GV1032.A1F668 2006   796.72092'2   C2006-906361-3

Project Director: J. Alexander Poulton

Cover & Title Page Images: Mark Thompson/Getty Images Sport

PC: P5

Dedication

This book is dedicated to veteran Canadian Formula One and Formula Atlantic racer Bill Brack, whose generosity and personal reminiscences made writing this book possible, allowing me a personal look inside the exciting world of F1.

Contents

Acknowledgments

I would like to express my gratitude to my friends and family who tolerated my single-mindedness as I spent hours researching old magazine and newspaper clippings, digging through years of long-forgotten race statistics, championship points standings and several gruesome crash reports. Thanks go out to fellow race fan and F1 photographer Franco Agostino, whose encouraging words always meant a great deal to me; to Irene Trester who always made sure my occasional writer's block was cured by a good refueling dinner at our favorite diner; and to Jacqueline Robichaud, who was always there to kick my rear bumper when I slowed down.

Introduction

Formula One auto racing was officially launched in 1950 with the Fédération Internationale de l'Automobile's (FIA's) standardization of rules. Its origins lie in the European Grand Prix(GP) motor racing of the 1920s and 1930s, and as an answer to the Motorcycle World Championships that were introduced in 1949, the FIA organized the first-ever official World Championship for Drivers using the Formula One rules in 1950. The championship then consisted of the six major Grands Prix of Europe plus the Indianapolis 500.

My first recollection of Formula One(F1) is from back in the late '50s when I was a little girl. I used to watch sportscasts of early races with my dad on a huge television console with a very tiny oval screen. I remember the exotic-sounding names of

Ferrari, Maserati and Alfa Romeo, as well as the not-so-foreign-sounding ones such as Moss, Hawthorn and Brabham.

I also remember writing a letter to Santa Claus (or Father Christmas, as he's known where I come from) asking for some new pencils, coloring books, plastic farmyard animals, a couple of favorite chocolate bars and a shiny new red Alfa Romero. Well, I got the pencils and books for school, and to this day I still have my plastic horses, cows and sheep, but hey, Santa…I'm still waiting for that Alfa!

In the late '60s and early '70s, I was a little more focused in my love of motorsports, especially when I discovered a groovy, sexy American driver called Peter Revson, heir to the Revlon fortune, jet-set playboy and driver of the hottest cars on the track—the Yardley-McLaren and the Shadow Ford (yes, I've also kept my faded pin-ups of Revson sitting in the cockpit of his McLaren). But my F1 passion cooled somewhat after his tragic death in 1974 during a practice session in South Africa. I then switched allegiances to the movies and devoted the rest of my young adulthood to worshiping safer idols such as Robert Redford, Paul Newman and the king of cool himself, Steve McQueen. At least Steve always survived his on-screen car chases, and *Bullitt* changed my life!

In recent years, though, Formula One has crept back into my heart and mind, especially with the new generation of talented drivers behind the wheel. We now have the GQ-style poster boys such as Alonso, Massa, Rosberg, Webber, Fisichella and Trulli, who not only drive brilliantly but look fabulous in their fire suits, too. We have accomplished technicians and strategists such as Coulthard, Räikkönen and Barrichello. And we have the new king of F1, Michael Schumacher, whose record-breaking run finally dethroned the legendary Fangio in early 2006.

But there is still a corner of my heart that holds dear the memories of those long-ago black and white newsreels of the great ones: Jackie Stewart, Stirling Moss, Ayrton Senna, Nigel Mansell, Nelson Piquet, Niki Lauda, Alain Prost...the list goes on. I hope the drivers profiled in this book make it on your list, too.

LEGENDS

Chapter One

Graham Hill

BIRTH DATE: **February 15, 1929**
BIRTHPLACE: **Hampstead, London, England**
DEATH DATE: **November 29, 1975**

---

*I'm an artist; the track is my canvas and the car
is my brush.*

—Graham Hill

What Johnny Depp is to pirates, Graham Hill was to Formula One racing. The most flamboyant, swashbuckling figure both on and off the track, complete with his trademark flowing hair and generous mustache, Graham Hill was the life and soul of any party. He was a larger than life man, always active and full of boundless energy, and he was the only driver ever to win auto racing's Triple Crown: the Indianapolis 500 (1966), the 24 Hours of Le Mans endurance race (1972) and the Formula One World Championship (twice—1962 and 1968). He was also a five-time winner of the prestigious Monaco Grand Prix (in 1963, 1964, 1965, 1968 and 1969).

When Hill died tragically in a 1975 air crash, the sports world lost a legend. Among the three thousand mourners attending his funeral in St Alban's, Hertfordshire, on December 5, were movie stars, politicians, pop stars and fans, so broad was Hill's appeal in the realm of celebrity.

Hill's was the classic rags-to-riches success story, which took place in the 1960s during Formula One's second decade of existence. He was extremely outgoing and was quite the dapper dandy who became the first F1 driver to become a media star, as comfortable making guest appearances on a television quiz show panel as he was behind the wheel of his race car. In 1953, he got his first intoxicating taste of car racing when he paid £1 to a newly formed racing school for a four-lap spin around England's famed Brands Hatch circuit in a 500cc Formula Three car. Since age 16, Hill had been working at Smiths Industries, the instrument makers, where he served a five-year apprenticeship before being called into the Navy. He returned to Smiths as a mechanic after a two-year stint at sea. At that time, his other great passion was rowing, but after those four laps his imagination was fired up, and he decided to pursue a career in motor racing.

At the school in Brands Hatch, called the Universal Motor Racing Club, Hill convinced the owner to allow him to exchange his labor as a mechanic for permission to drive one of the race cars. Unfortunately, the owner saw the naive Hill coming and took full advantage of the young man. The owner soon departed without Hill ever getting close to driving a race car. But Hill did not give up on his dream and soon entered into a similar arrangement with yet another new acquaintance; this time he actually got a chance to do some racing and soon, taking advantage of Hill's limited success, the new school had its first group of students. As Graham was the "veteran" (after only a handful of races), he became their instructor because the school's only other employee was also the owner!

Graham joined Team Lotus in the mid-'50s as a mechanic, and finally, at the unusually late age of nearly 30, he started racing. Through judicious socializing and plain hard work, Graham had finally made inroads into the auto-racing establishment. He struck up a relationship with Lotus boss Colin Chapman, with whom he had hitched a free ride back to London after both had raced at a regional event. The conversation must have been quite interesting, because almost immediately Hill started working at Lotus as a mechanic and was paid £1 per day, but he was unable to convince Chapman to give him a chance to race one of Chapman's cars. Hill quit Lotus temporarily before finally convincing Chapman to let him get behind the wheel. Graham's enthusiasm and unwavering work ethic eventually got him elevated to full-time driver, and in 1958, he made his debut in Formula One at Monaco. In 2006, without a couple of million pounds (or dollars) of guaranteed sponsorship and personal financing in his back pocket, no driver could ever manage such a feat.

It wasn't until Hill switched over to Bristish Racing Motors (BRM) in 1960 that real success appeared within reach. The BRM team had been in trouble for much of the 1950s, despite substantial financial support from the Owen Organization, but the development of a new V8 engine for the 1.5-liter F1 from 1961 onward raised the team's hopes considerably. After limited success and many mechanical failures with the Lotus team, Hill decided that a move to the more successful BRM team would offer him more opportunities to develop his skills and reach the podium. He almost won the British Grand Prix at Silverstone when he led the closing stages until spinning off under pressure from Jack Brabham in his Cooper, who then went on to win the race. By 1962, Hill had won his first race at Zandvoort and went on to claim the World Championship. Hill was also part of the other pre-Beatle "British invasion" of drivers at the Indianapolis 500 during the mid-1960s, triumphing there in 1966 in a Lola-Ford.

Graham continued to notch up victories at Monaco between 1963 and 1965, and he just failed to capture the 1964 title after being knocked out of contention in the Mexican GP by Ferrari driver Lorenzo Bandini. In 1965, he was joined at BRM by newcomer Jackie Stewart. The young upstart upstaged Hill, who then caused a sensation in F1 circles when he joined his old rival Jimmy Clark and Mike Spence at Team Lotus in 1967. The creation of this "super team" was actually a Ford-financed effort to assemble the strongest possible driving team in preparation for the arrival of the new Lotus 49 with its Cosworth DFV V8 engine, financed by the American motor giant.

After both Spence and Clark died tragically in 1968 at Hockenheim, Graham Hill scored victories in the Spanish, Monaco and Mexican GPs, enough to ease Jackie Stewart out of the championship title. But the Lotus had a reputation of being very fragile and dangerous during this period, especially with the new aerodynamic aids that caused similar crashes for Hill and Jochen Rindt at the 1969 Spanish Grand Prix.

Although he scored a win at Monaco (his fifth triumph on the difficult Monaco circuit, a record that was not surpassed until Ayrton Senna captured his sixth victory in 1993) 1969 was not a good year for Hill. At the U.S. Grand Prix at Watkins Glen, Hill was injured in a terrible accident that left him confined to a wheelchair. He smashed both legs when he was thrown from his car after tire failure, but his determination and focus on recovery got him back behind the wheel in time to win a Championship point in the South African Grand Prix at Kyalami in 1970. His son, Damon, also a brilliant racer, inherited the family trait of raising his game in deepest adversity, a trait that has been tested many times.

Chapman was upset by Hill's accident, but no amount of sentimentality would cloud his judgment—Graham Hill was now past his prime. For the 1970 season, Chapman secured Hill a ride in a private Lotus fielded by Rob Walker, and Graham fought bravely to sustain his reputation, switching to Brabham for the 1971 and 1972 seasons and starting his own team in 1973—known as Embassy Hill—with sponsorship from Embassy cigarettes. The team used chassis from Shadow and Lola before introducing its own design in 1975, a private Shadow DN1. Despite a heroic push forward, Hill endured a disappointing 1974 season, and when he failed to qualify at Monaco in 1975, there was no disputing that it was time to hang up the helmet.

His last win in Formula One had been the non-championship International Trophy at Silverstone in 1971 with the Brabham BT42 "Lobster claw" car. Then, in 1972, he teamed with Henri Pescarolo, he won the 24 Hours of Le Mans for Matra.

At the 1975 British Grand Prix, Hill announced his retirement after a record 176 Grand Prix starts, 14 victories and two World Championships, stating he would concentrate on developing the career of his brilliant, newly signed driver, Tony Brise. Grand Prix racing's most famous senior citizen was about to commence an active, yet comfortable, retirement with the prospect of growing old with dignity alongside his wife Bette, whom he wed in 1955, and their children Bridget, Samantha and Damon.

But fate dealt the 46-year-old legend a vicious last hand when the private plane he was piloting from Marseilles, France, went down after getting lost in the fog over Arkley, Hertfordshire, on November 29, 1975. Hill was killed instantly along with the four other occupants in his Piper Aztec— Ray Brimble, fellow driver Tony Brise and two mechanics, all members of the Embassy Hill team. Hill was piloting the plane himself when it clipped a row of trees bordering the Arkley golf course.

Visibility had been poor at the time of the accident, and the ambulances and other emergency rescuers couldn't even see the bunkers as they were rushing to the crash site. An inquest found Hill was flying only 60 feet above the ground when the plane hit the tree, but he was not aware of this lack of altitude because of the poor visibility. Verdicts of accidental death were returned for all six occupants of the plane; however, it was later revealed that Hill had not properly insured the plane, and the bereaved families had no alternative but to sue his estate for financial compensation

Behind Graham Hill's seemingly ebullient public demeanor lurked a less-than-charitable side. Away from his adoring fans and public scrutiny, he was often rude and extremely irresponsible, taking chances that might jeopardize those around him. But on the day of his funeral, all that was forgotten. Memories of the dashing racer tearing around the race circuits in his jaunty jalopy filled hearts and minds, as did the image of his famous Hill helmet with the rowing stripes. In 1993, Graham's son Damon, himself a legend in the making, resurrected that famous icon in Formula One, donning a helmet bearing the famous insignia.

In 1990, Graham Hill was inducted into the International Motorsports Hall of Fame, forever to remain in Formula One's collective consciousness.

Chapter Two

Mario Andretti

BIRTH DATE: February 20, 1940
BIRTHPLACE: Montona D'Istria, Italy
RESIDES: Nazareth, Pennsylvania, U.S.A.

Over the years, there have been a number of drivers who have attempted to cross over from one racing format to another, but few, if any, have achieved the resounding success and acclaim in NASCAR, Indy and Formula One that Mario Andretti has.

Heading up one of the most successful and well-known racing dynasties, Mario has become a one-man industry unto himself since retiring from active racing. He is a highly respected product spokesman for his sponsors, appearing regularly on television in public service announcements concerning driver safety. He is also the owner of a famous driving school for would-be racers and has become a successful vineyard owner and wine expert.

Andretti, an Italian immigrant who came to North America to achieve fame and fortune in a job he would have gladly done for free, personifies the "American Dream." This congenial man of action possesses a natural talent that brought him success in so many types of racing, including realizing his boyhood ambition of becoming Formula One World Champion.

Mario and his twin brother, Aldo, were born in Montona, a town near the Italian port city of Trieste, on February 20, 1940, in the midst of World War II. The Andretti family spent the first seven years of the boys' lives in a camp for displaced persons, enduring crowded conditions and severe food shortages. When the war ended, that region of Italy was given over to the Communists and became part of what was then Yugoslavia. The Andrettis moved to the town of Lucca, where young Mario first became aware of auto racing. It was the start of his all-consuming passion.

The awestruck brothers delighted in watching the famous *Mille Miglia*, the thousand-mile road race that passed through Lucca each year, but what really captured Mario's imagination was his visit to the 1954 Italian Grand Prix at Monza. He watched and listened as the Lancia, Maserati and Ferrari Formula One cars whizzed by, and he was held spellbound by the heroic exploits of drivers such as Juan-Manuel Fangio and Alberto Ascari. It was Ascari who became Mario's idol, and even after Italy's great champion was killed at Monza in 1955, Ascari remained Mario's inspiration and role model.

In 1955, the Andretti family set sail for America in search of a better life, and for both Aldo and Mario, this involved car racing around their new home of Nazareth, Pennsylvania. The boys were just 18 when they started competing on dangerous dirt track ovals behind the wheel of a self-built Hudson Hornet they shared at stock car events. In 1959, during one of these races, Aldo crashed and suffered serious injuries. He never raced again. But Mario kept right on racing as often as possible, even as many as five races a day, building upon each success. He tore up dirt tracks across the Midwest in all sorts of sprint cars and midgets, and although he remained a fair and honorable racer, the aggressive, competitive environment forced the normally easy-going Andretti to transform himself into an intimidating foe on the track.

Andretti conquered the giant stock car speedways, becoming the United States Auto Club (USAC) Champion several times and winning the legendary Indianapolis. His versatile, transferable driving skills brought about more success when he won the 1967 Daytona 500, his first stock car race in which he led the race for 112 laps, including the final 33. This was only his seventh Grand National career start in NASCAR. He also triumphed at the Sebring 12-Hour race for sports cars, yet he longed to compete in his first love: Formula One.

After a 1965 race at Indianapolis, where he had secured a one-off ride finishing third behind the winning Lotus driven by Jim Clark, Andretti was promised a future drive by famed Lotus boss, Colin Chapman. Finally, in 1968, Andretti made his sensational Formula One debut in the U.S. Grand Prix at Watkins Glen, qualifying his Lotus 49 in the pole position. Chapman was then prepared to offer him a full-time drive, replacing Clark, who had been killed earlier that year, but Andretti was unwilling to abandon the security of his lucrative career in American stock car racing and only agreed to occasional Formula One events that his USAC commitments allowed.

Over the next few years, Mario made a number of Formula One appearances but drove in uncompetitive Lotus, March and Parnelli cars. In 1971, he signed with Ferrari to drive in the sports cars series (winning several races with co-driver Jacky Ickx) and in Formula One, where he won the season's first Grand Prix in South Africa. Following this taste of success, Mario experienced a lean period in his USAC career that prompted him to finally concentrate on Formula One racing in 1976, although his decision to join the then-faltering Team Lotus seemed an unlikely route to any Grand Prix glory.

Andretti endured a volatile relationship with Lotus boss Chapman that saw many fiery arguments on the track and in the garage, but the two men were eventually able to develop a productive partnership. Though Mario struggled with Chapman's frightening, unpredictable Lotus 77, he managed to score a momentous victory in the final race of 1976, the Japanese Grand Prix at Fuji. This was Lotus' first win in five years, and Chapman was inspired to greater efforts on the drawing board. Mario won 4 races in Chapman's pioneering 1977 creation, the Lotus 78 ground effect car that Andretti had a hand in developing. In 1978, with six victories—five of which were in the innovative Lotus 79—Mario Andretti became World Champion, his dream come true.

The steam ran out of the Chapman/Andretti partnership as Chapman lost his way on the drawing board, creating cars that were consistently under performing. Following two unproductive seasons, Andretti packed his gear and moved over to Alfa Romeo. Again, he was forced to endure two years of poor performances from less-than-perfect cars.

He eventually left Formula One racing to concentrate on racing in Indy and stock cars, but the siren's call of F1 was loud. Mario could not resist the invitation extended by Enzo Ferrari to make one final guest appearance at the 1982 Italian Grand Prix in Monza. There, at the circuit where he

first caught F1 fever as an impressionable youngster, the weathered, 42-year-old veteran qualified
his Ferrari 126 Turbo on the pole and drove flat out
to an impressive third. He finally closed the F1
books with an impressive record comprised of 128
GP starts, 12 wins and 18 poles.

From 1961 until 2000, Andretti competed in
over 870 multi-format races, winning 111 of them
and taking 109 pole positions. He was crowned
Driver of the Century by the Associated Press in
1999, tying with AJ Foyt for the title. *Racer* magazine awarded him a similar title in 2000, and then
they dubbed him the Greatest American Driver
Ever in 2002. He has parlayed his fame and
considerable fortune into a number of racing
businesses, including a driving school, several car
dealerships and a petroleum company, but his vine-
yards in Napa, California, are winning him even
more accolades: *Wine Business Monthly* (February
2006 edition) named the Andretti Winery as one
of the Top Ten Hottest Small Brands in 2005.

His passion for racing, though, keeps him close
to the track, as does his family, with a third generation of Andrettis now firmly entrenched in
the business. Mario's grandson Marco, the son of
former open-wheel racing champ and two-time
Indy Car Series Championship–winning team
owner, Michael, has been involved in racing
since he was nine years old. In 2003, Marco

finished a successful first season in open-wheel cars, with an Eastern Series Championship title coming the following year. Marco placed fifth in the 2005 Star Mazda Championship and won three of his six races in his debut for the Menards Infiniti Pro Series. "My grandson will always be reason for me to be trackside," boasts proud grandpa Mario. "There have been a number of TV documentaries made about my life and career, as well as several books. But there are still a few chapters left for the Andrettis to write." And for sure, the Andretti patriarch will still be found trackside offering advice and directing traffic, ensuring his racing legacy continues well into the 21st century.

Chapter Three

Gilles Villeneuve

BIRTH DATE: January 18, 1950
BIRTHPLACE: Richelieu, Quebec, Canada
DEATH DATE: May 8, 1982

Canadian Joseph Gilles Henri Villeneuve was one the most exciting, world-renowned Formula One racing drivers in modern history. Raised in the small town of Berthierville, Québec, he won his first F1 race in his home country at the 1978 Canadian Grand Prix, held in Montreal. Even though he had a short career, he won six Grand Prix races and finished second in the 1979 championship, only four points behind teammate Jody Scheckter.

Gilles started competing in regional snowmobile races at the age of 17, thanks to the help and support of the local Skiroule dealer in Berthierville, and by 1972, he had joined the Moto-Ski snowmobile team. By then, he had married Joann Barthe and had become a father to Jacques, who would himself go on to racing fame.

By 1973, Gilles had started establishing a name for himself as a bit of a daredevil, tempered only by the birth of his second child, a daughter named Mélanie. He finally broke into the Formula Ford series, landing the Rookie of the Year title and winning the Quebec Championship.

Gilles continued racing snowmobiles throughout 1974, winning the World Championship at Eagle River, Wisconsin. In the warmer months of that year, he began racing in the Atlantic Formula with the Ecurie Canada racing team, scoring his first win in 1975 at Gimli, Manitoba. Throughout 1976, he notched up more victories, with 9 wins out of 10 starts in the Atlantic Formula, claiming championships in both Canada and the U.S. He also ran his first race on European soil in Formula Two at Pau, France.

Gilles' first Formula One outing was in 1977 at Silverstone, England, and the same year, he claimed his second Canadian Championship title while scoring his 13th victory in the Atlantic Formula. Finally, in September, he got the call from Ferrari, and as his signature was drying on his contract, the entire family packed up and moved to Cannes, France.

In less than a year, Gilles scored his first victory in Formula One at the Canadian Grand Prix in October, and the family moved yet again, this time to the Principality of Monaco.

The wins started coming fast and furious. Gilles' second victory was at the Kyalami Grand Prix in South Africa. His third win came the following April at the Long Beach Grand Prix in California. By October, the Watkins Glen, NY, GP had fallen to the French-Canadian four-wheeled wizard.

Villeneuve will always be remembered for his wild driving technique, especially during his wheel-banging duel with René Arnoux in the last laps of the 1979 French Grand Prix, considered one of the most intense, thrilling moments in Formula One racing. Despite this, his six Grand Prix wins represent some of the most mechanically sensitive and tactically astute in the history of the sport. Perhaps his greatest season was 1981, when he managed to wrestle his unwieldy turbo Ferrari to victory at Monaco then followed that with a classic exhibition of defensive driving in Spain where he kept five quicker cars behind him using his superb tactical acumen and his car's superior straight-line speed.

Gilles Villeneuve started the 1982 season as the obvious favorite for the championship crown. By then, he was widely regarded as the best Formula One driver in the field, and after two years of medi-ocre cars, Ferrari finally produced a competitive package. After some near-misses in the opening races, Villeneuve got back in form for the San Marino Grand Prix, but teammate Didier Pironi disobeyed the crew bosses' orders to relinquish the

lead to Villeneuve and beat him to the line. Villeneuve claimed that he was merely coasting going
into the final laps, knowing that victory was in the
bag and trusting his teammate to allow him to
pass. After this betrayal, an angry Villeneuve
vowed never to speak to Pironi again…and he
never did.

Sadly, Villeneuve never made it to another
checkered flag. On May 8, 1982, while qualifying
for the Belgian Grand Prix, Villeneuve's car hit the
right rear wheel of Jochen Mass's car as Mass was
driving at a slower pace along the inside of the
track. The impact was so great that Villeneuve's
car was sent airborne and spun nose over tail along
the track's soft embankment. When the car finally
came to rest, the chassis was completely ripped
apart. The driver's seat landed across the track in
the catchfence with the lifeless driver still strapped
in. Emergency crews rushed to his side; however,
Villeneuve was pronounced dead shortly after he
reached the hospital. The force of the initial impact
had killed him instantly.

Gilles Villeneuve's funeral at Berthierville was
attended by many of his fellow racers, as well as
fans and media who not only mourned his
untimely loss but also celebrated his legend. Jodie
Scheckter, his former teammate, delivered the
eulogy: "I will miss Gilles for two reasons. First, he
was the fastest driver in the history of motor racing.

Second, he was the most genuine man I have ever known. But he has gone. The memory of what he has done, what he has achieved, will always be there."

Today, more than two decades after his death, the fans still remember, as do sports industry insiders. Ferrari erected a bronze bust of Villeneuve at the entrance to their test track, and the Imola track dubbed one of its most dangerous corners "Curva Gilles." In 1982, Montreal renamed its famed racetrack on Ile Notre-Dame (home to the Canadian Grand Prix) for Villeneuve, and 10 years later, the Gilles Villeneuve racing museum at Berthierville opened, and a statue was unveiled in a nearby park that also bears his name.

Gilles Villeneuve was inducted into the Canadian Motorsport Hall of Fame during its inaugural induction ceremonies in Toronto in 1993, and in June 1997, Canada issued a postage stamp to honor its favorite racing son.

Villeneuve's spectacular driving is considered an art form among serious Formula One fans. As Niki Lauda, whom Gilles replaced in 1977 as a member of the Ferrari team, assesses: "Gilles was the perfect racing driver...with the best talent of all of us." This is an opinion shared by many other Grand Prix drivers and veteran journalists who have covered the sport.

Like other legendary racers, such as Clark and Senna, Villeneuve had a curious mixture of character traits. A little crazy, a little smart, even a little sensitive. Whether he was flying, snowmobiling or driving, he was a risk-taker of classic proportions. Yet according to his fellow drivers on the track, he was scrupulously fair and never put anyone's safety—other than his own—in jeopardy. This made him exceptionally popular, not only with fans, but with teammates and opponents as well.

Gilles' brother Jacques, known as "Uncle" Jacques, also had a successful racing career, winning the Formula Atlantic and Can Am series championships as well as becoming the first Canadian to win a race in the Championship Auto Racing Teams(CART) series. "Uncle" Jacques joined his brother in the Canadian Motorsport Hall of Fame in 2001.

Chapter Four

Stirling Moss

BIRTH DATE: September 17, 1929
BIRTHPLACE: Batesville, Arizona, U.S.A.
RESIDES: London, England

When I was a little girl tearing around our family yard on my tricycle, I remember on more than one occasion my father laughing and telling me to slow down. "Who do you think you are? Stirling Moss?"

For many years, both during and after Moss' career, that was the standard question asked by many a British police officer when pulling over speeding motorists. The legendary racer relates that he himself was once stopped for speeding and asked that very question, and Sir Stirling Moss still smiles when he recalls the difficulty the traffic officer had believing him. "Oh, you ARE Stirling Moss!"

Sir Stirling Moss is arguably the greatest all-round racing driver of all time, and without doubt, he was the greatest driver who never won the

World Championship. Known during his career as "Mr. Motor Racing," Moss was a pioneer on the British Formula One racing scene.

The Moss family was quite involved in auto racing. Stirling's father, Alfred, studied in the U.S. shortly after WW I, often competing in friendly races with fellow students and even placing 14th at the 1924 Indianapolis 500. Stirling's mother also raced in rallies and time trials back home in the UK, and younger sister, Pat, was a keen fan of the sport, eventually marrying rally racer Erik Carlsson.

By the time Stirling turned nine, Alfred had bought him an old Austin Seven jalopy, in which the youngster would drive around the fields surrounding their home. Although motorsports were a family pastime, Stirling was forced to choose a proper career, and it was thought that he would follow his dad's footsteps, becoming a dentist and eventually taking over the lucrative family business. But his less-than-impressive scholastic achievements made that impossible. So at age 17, Stirling decided to enter the hotel business. His training included serving as a waiter and a night porter, but these occupations totally bored him. Soon the roar of engines beckoned, and the family agreed he should do what he loved best—race cars. So in 1948, at age 18, he started hill climb races in a Cooper 500, where he excelled, and he was soon driving works cars for Jaguar and Hersham & Walton Motors (HWM).

In 1950, Moss secured his first works team drive for HWM. Created by John Heath and George Abecassis, partners in HWM, the team was comprised of three four-cylinder Formula Two cars. The team became a legend in British auto racing history, with Moss partnering with team leader Lance Macklin and chief mechanic Kovaleski, a Polish ex-serviceman who later adopted the English name Alf Francis. Moss' record with HWM was uninspiring to say the least, with cars breaking down more often then not, but the fledgling speedster remembers this period as a great learning experience. During his time at HWM, he also raced other cars, including the Jaguar C-Type, in which he won the sports car race leading up to the French Grand Prix. This was the first win for a car using disk brakes.

Moss was contracted to race for Ferrari at selected events in 1951, but when practice began for the first race in Bari, Italy, he was told unceremoniously that the car he had assumed was his had been given to the more experienced driver Taruffi. Moss was embarrassed by Ferrari's lack of confidence in his skills and vowed to prove his worth; little did anyone realize that in the process, Stirling Moss would become a legend.

In 1955 he was signed up by Mercedes-Benz to partner World Champion Juan-Manuel Fangio, but almost immediately, Stirling was matching the great Argentine in most Grands Prix, eventually beating him in the British GP. Moss made history that same year when he won the incredible *Mille Miglia*, the *Targa Florio* and the Tourist Trophy—all legendary sports car races. In the *Mille Miglia*—the Italian 1000-mile open-road endurance race—Moss won in record time, finishing more than 10 hours ahead of second-place finisher, Fangio. His co-driver in the Mercedes-Benz 300 SLR was British journalist Denis Jenkinson, who supported Moss with topographical and geographical details of the long road ahead. This was an innovative technique among rallying co-drivers at the time. Jenkinson's assistance helped Moss compete against European contenders who possessed a large amount of local knowledge of the gruelling route.

Moss' first Formula One victory came in 1955 at his home race, the British GP at Aintree. He was behind the wheel of the outstanding Mercedes-Benz W196 Monoposto for this, the only race where he finished in front of teammate and friend Fangio, who was his mentor and archrival at Mercedes. The legitimacy of the win has been a subject of debate for many years. Many have suggested that Fangio, one of the greatest "gentlemen" of the sport may have intentionally slowed to allow Moss to pass and take the flag in front of his home fans. However, according to Moss, Fangio assured him that Moss was the better driver that day and truly earned the win.

The daunting 25-kilometer Pescara Circuit is the longest circuit ever to host a Grand Prix, and in 1957 Moss demonstrated his skill at high speed and long distance driving over the three-hour course when he beat out Fangio, who started on the pole, by a little over three minutes.

Moss raced from 1948 to 1962, winning 194 of the 497 races he entered, including 16 Formula One GPs. He once told an interviewer that he had participated in 525 races in total, as many as 62 in a single year in 84 different cars. He is considered by many to be the first modern professional driver who raced for the love of the sport, but he was also well aware of the potential for earning a sizable income. Moss stayed in top physical shape and traveled all over the world to race. Like many drivers from this early era, he competed in several formulas, switching between cars and teams several times a week.

For four years in a row (1955–58) Moss placed second in the World Championship, and after Mercedes-Benz retired, he led the Maserati and Vanwall teams. He also continued to drive touring and sports cars; in fact, throughout this remarkable career, Moss drove over 80 different types of car. He drove a private Jaguar and raced for Maserati,

Vanwall, Lotus, Cooper and Briggs Cunningham, as well as the famed Mercedes-Benz. But he preferred racing in British cars, which were often uncompetitive and were considered to be the reason he never won the Drivers' Championship.

Moss was renowned for his impeccable manners on track, much like friend and rival Fangio. But his sportsmanship and generosity may have cost him the World Championship in 1958 when he defended the integrity of another driver, Mike Hawthorn, during a race in Portugal.

During the race, Hawthorn spun his car but was able to continue and eventually finished second to Moss with a one-point difference in championship scoring. Before they all took to the podium, Hawthorn was accused by race officials of breaking the rules by restarting in the opposite direction. Moss had witnessed the incident and quickly came to his rival's defense, and a relieved Hawthorn was able to keep his race points. Moss lost the championship that year to Hawthorn by a single point, even though he had thoroughly beaten his fellow countryman 4–1 in race wins. Would any of today's racers take this high road under similar circumstances? Dear readers...place your bets. It would not be Schumacher!

Throughout the late '50s and early '60s, Moss led the changeover to rear-engined F1 cars, achieving the first victory for such a car at the 1958

Argentine GP. Moss was indeed in a class of his own during this period; however, a near-fatal accident ended it all in 1962 when he was badly injured in a crash at Goodwood, England, while driving a Lotus. He recovered and attempted a somewhat premature comeback but found he was not fit enough to withstand the rigors of professional racing. Moss wisely decided to retire from GP racing, although he continued to race historic cars at celebrity events and promotional outings.

Although Moss failed to win a championship throughout his auspicious career, this in no way diminishes the impact his achievements had on the sport. Moss was at home in any type of car on any type of track or road. When he and Denis Jenkinson won the 1955 *Mille Miglia*, they were the first "foreigners" and the only Britons to ever do so.

One of the original jet-setters, Moss continued traveling around the world, fulfilling engagements and competing in historic racing events well into his 70s, and he has written several books about his life behind the wheel. In 1990, Stirling Moss was inducted into the elite International Motorsports Hall of Fame, and in June 2005, in an appearance at the Goodwood Revival, he signed the hood of his 1955 *Mille Miglia*–winning Mercedes-Benz 300 SLR, which was donated to the Mercedes-Benz museum in Stuttgart.

Also in the summer of 2005, a life-sized bronze statue commemorating Sir Stirling's life and accomplishments was unveiled at the historic Mallory Park racing circuit in Leicestershire, England. Many of the more than 80 cars in which Moss had competed throughout the years were present at the ceremony, brought to the event from around the British Isles and Europe by their private owners. One of the cars on display was the #20 Lotus 18 that Moss had driven to one of his most exciting victories of all, the 1961 Monaco GP when he famously had the side panels removed to aid cooling.

In his day, Stirling Moss was a trendsetter who helped pave the way for the huge sponsorship contracts that have allowed the F1 to blossom into a leading spectator sport in the 21st century. He had courted endorsements like no other driver of his day and was often ridiculed for this entrepreneurial concept, but in truth, he was just way ahead of his time.

Now enjoying a more serene lifestyle, Moss currently resides with his wife in sunny Florida, but he continues to follow Formula One and other forms of four-wheeled racing.

Chapter Five

Ayrton Senna

BIRTH DATE: March 21, 1960

BIRTHPLACE: São Paulo, Brazil

DEATH DATE: May 1, 1994

It's going to be a season with lots of accidents, and I'll risk saying that we'll be lucky if something really serious doesn't happen.
      –A. Senna, pre-1994 season

Brazilian Ayrton Senna was indeed a legend in his own lifetime. He made 161 Grand Prix starts, scored 41 Grand Prix victories and 65 GP Pole Positions and won three F1 World Championships. More than 10 years after his untimely and tragic death, he is still considered by many as the greatest driver in F1 history. Senna was a spectacularly talented driver, strong-willed, forceful and unyielding, seldom appearing vulnerable behind the wheel. His character, life, career and the circumstances of his death approach what could arguably be termed mythical; he was a complex character who fascinated race fans the world over. Many of his fans still mourn his death, particularly those in Brazil.

Ayrton Senna da Silva was born on March 21, 1960, in São Paulo, Brazil, and as a child, showed little signs of a career in any sort of sport, let alone racing. In fact, he was a completely uncoordinated youngster. To help his son, Senna's father, Milton, purchased a small one-horsepower kart for his four-year-old boy, and from that day onwards, Ayrton never looked back. In Brazil, youngsters are not legally allowed to race in any motorized vehicle until the age of 13. So, after nine years of practice, Ayrton won his first competitive race on July 1, 1973. Within a few years, Senna was winning championship titles (1977–81), proving once and for all just how well coordinated he had become.

Heading off to Europe in 1981, Senna entered the British Formula Ford 1600 competition, which he won. He also adopted his mother's maiden name, Senna, partly because da Silva is a common name in Brazil but also because his name was too long for the pit boards. At this point, Senna's father tried to convince Ayrton to give up racing; money was in short supply, and this was long before the big sponsorship deals we have come to know. All of Senna's attempts to gain financial backing had failed, so in October that same year, he announced that he would retire and head back to Brazil. But life did not improve; after spending four months managing his father's building company, Senna's passion for racing had grown even stronger. His father gave him a choice: the family business or racing. Not surprisingly, Senna chose racing.

With his career back on track in 1982, Senna quickly won the British and the European Formula Ford 2000 Championships, as well as the prestigious, high profile Macau Grand Prix. Out of 27 races, he achieved 16 poles, 23 fastest laps and 22 wins. At his first-ever Formula Three event, Senna out-qualified the field, set the fastest lap time and subsequently won the race. It was a sign of great things to come.

In the 1983 British F3 championship, Senna was victorious, and after testing with the Williams, McLaren, Brabham and Toleman teams, he secured a ride with the Toleman organization in time for the 1984 Formula One season.

The Toleman team was comparatively small, but despite this, the team produced a competitive car powered by Hart Turbo engines. This was to be Senna's chariot as he started his meteoric rise to the top of the podium and immortality.

He scored his first World Championship point on April 7, 1984, at the South African Grand Prix, followed soon after by the Monaco GP, where rain plagued the event. Senna started 13th on the grid but soon picked his way through the wet field. By lap 19, he had already passed the second place Niki Lauda and was on his way to chasing down the leader, Alain Prost. But the rain started pouring down like a monsoon, and on lap 31 the race was stopped, giving Senna his first podium finish. Two more podium finishes (thirds) followed at the British GP at Brands Hatch and at the season-ending Portuguese GP at Estoril, ultimately giving Senna ninth place in the standings, tied at 13 points with Nigel Mansell.

After he joined Lotus in 1985, Senna took seven pole positions and won at the Portugal and Belgium GPs. The 1986 season gave him eight poles, with victories in Spain and the U.S. Going into 1987, Senna negotiated a three-year contract with McLaren-Honda while he finished his last season at Lotus. He ranked third in the championship points standing.

In 1988, he partnered with World Champion driver Alain Prost over at McLaren, where the young Brazilian upstart eclipsed Prost with 13 pole positions, 8 GP wins and his first World Championship title.

The volatile relationship between the two teammates came to a head in Japan in 1989. Senna started from pole, but Prost beat him into the first corner and stayed out front for most of the race. Then, with only six laps left, Senna made his move, coming alongside Prost, who refused to concede as they both turned into the corner. The two cars collided and came to an abrupt halt, with Prost leaving his car. Senna remained in the cockpit, and race marshals were able to push-start his McLaren. He managed to retake the lead to win the race. Unfortunately, an outraged Senna was later disqualified for missing the chicane. With Senna's loss of points, Prost won the World Championship that year and, fortunately for all, moved on to join Ferrari for the 1990 season.

In 1990 and 1991, Senna won back-to-back championship titles, all the time battling with Prost and Nigel Mansell. But the loss of Honda power and the rise of Renault would eventually bring about the decline of McLaren, and in 1992, Senna finished fourth in the championship, having taken only one pole position and three wins.

The frustration started showing, and Senna considered taking a time off to sit out the 1993 season. The McLaren team, however, was persuasive and both parties settled on a pay-by-race deal. Senna continued to dominate and, in his last drive for McLaren, made them the most successful Formula One team in history, with a record 104 wins. He performed spectacularly in his outmatched McLaren MP 4/8, winning a total of five GPs for the season. The most impressive and perhaps the finest victory of his career was at the European GP, where Senna won after picking up five places in the rain on the first lap, cementing his place in history as the "king of the wet." He ended the season as runner-up in the World Championship and looked forward to a new season, a new winning car and a fresh challenge over at the Williams team.

Ayrton Senna landed one of the richest deals to date in F1, striking a $20 million per-year deal with the Williams team, the same team who had given him his first test ride in an F1 car more than a decade earlier. Senna had wanted to return to Williams for a long time, and at one point he had even offered to drive for them for free.

The new season began with great promise for Senna, but tragedy struck at Imola as he was leading the restarted San Marino GP. His FW16B suddenly veered off the track inexplicably, crossing over the grass verge and concrete run-off area before finally impacting with a concrete wall on the Tamburello bend. On Sunday May 1, 1994, with millions of race fans watching via television, the world lost one of its greatest sportsmen.

The beginning of the '94 season had already taken the life of Roland Ratzberger, the young Austrian driver, and Rubens Barrichello suffered a near-fatal crash during a practice run. Now the fans watched as the seemingly immortal Senna struggled for survival in the hands of the on-track medical team. Although many witnesses claim to have seen Senna's head move, doctors eventually confirmed that when the unconscious driver's eyes were tested, the pupils indicated he had suffered severe head trauma. Once his body was extracted from the cockpit and laid on the ground, there were no signs of life in the 34-year-old legend.

Track officials immediately closed rank and released little information to the public regarding the crash. What eventually became known, though, was that the front right tire and suspension equipment became detached and flew back, hitting Senna directly in the head, piercing his helmet visor. This apparently was the cause of the trauma and massive brain injury. Telemetric studies indicated that Senna had been traveling at approximately 193 mph when the Tamburello accident occurred and had been able to drop his speed to 135 mph in less than two seconds. But even this amazing feat of driving skill was not enough to prevent or lessen the impact.

After Senna's death, Brazil was plunged into three days of official mourning for its national hero, and an estimated one million people lined the streets in tribute as his funeral procession passed by. He was interred at the Cemitério do Morumbi in his hometown of São Paulo.

Tamburello will always be remembered as the final corner in Ayrton Senna's career. The name is whispered in hushed tones by racing aficionados. After Senna's accident, the Autodromo Enzo e Dino Ferrari racetrack in Imola was immediately investigated by the FIA, along with the Tamburello. The corner had long been controversial because it had no run-off, and it was the site of two previous incidents: Nelson Piquet's 1987 crash, resulting from tire failure, and two years later, Gerhard Berger's wreck, in which his Ferrari flamed out after a tire and front wing failure early in the race. Berger survived the Tamburello thanks to the alert safety workers, but after Senna's death, the sweeper corner was replaced by a chicane in 1995.

To this day, the FIA and Italian authorities still maintain that Senna was not killed instantly but rather died in hospital after an emergency tracheotomy and IV were administered trackside and en route in the helicopter. There has been much debate as to why Senna was not declared dead at the track; however, under Italian law when a person dies at any sporting event, that death must be investigated and the event cancelled.

Ironically, the weekend of his death, Senna had been extremely upset by the Ratzberger and Barichello crashes. Although doctors barred anyone other than family from visiting, Senna jumped a rear security wall to visit Barrichello in the hospital. When Ratzenberger lost his life, the FIA was forced to reconsider the safety issue and Senna considered retiring on the spot. Senna had great respect for his competitors, and when he died, doctors found an Austrian flag in his car. Senna was sure he would win, and he wanted to show his respect for Ratzenberger.

Senna was convinced that safety standards needed to be reviewed. He spent his final morning participating in discussions with fellow drivers, determined to take on the new responsibility of creating an updated Drivers' Safety group and looking at necessary safety changes for F1. Being the most senior driver on the circuit at that time, he was asked to take on the role of leader in this effort.

Because he was a very private man off-track, it wasn't until after Senna's death that the public learned just how humane and compassionate he was. In 1992 at Spa-Francorchamps in Belgium, Erik Comas had crashed heavily on the back straight during a free practice session. All the other drivers drove past Comas' wreckage at high speed, but Senna jumped out of his car and, endangering his own life, sprinted back down the track to the wrecked car and reached inside to hit the electrics kill switch, preventing a possible fire and sure death for Comas.

In 1993 at Spa-Francorchamps when Alessandro Zanardi crashed his Lotus at the Eau Rouge corner, Senna was again seen jumping from his car to help the injured driver.

After Senna's death, it was also discovered that he had donated millions of dollars to children's charities, a fact he had kept secret during his life. In his honor, the Senna family created the Ayrton Senna Foundation, an organization that helps poor and needy young people in Brazil and around the world.

Senna was posthumously inducted into the International Motorsports Hall of Fame in 2000.

On April 21, 2004, to mark the 10th anniversary of Senna's passing, over 10,000 people attended a charity soccer match in a stadium near Imola. The game was organized by several of Ayrton's devoted Italian and Canadian fans, and it brought together the 1994 Brazilian national soccer team team to face the Nazionale Piloti, an exhibition team made up exclusively of top race car drivers. Michael Schumacher, Jarno Trulli, Rubens Barrichello, Fernando Alonso and many others faced members of the team that won the World Cup in the U.S. 10 years earlier.

Chapter Six

Bill Brack

BIRTH DATE: December 26, 1935

BIRTHPLACE: Toronto, Ontario, Canada

RESIDES: Dunnville, Ontario, Canada

Canadian all-round racer, William "Bill" Brack was born in Toronto, Ontario, and originally started racing Minis in the early 1960s over frozen lakes that had enough ice thickness to safely carry the weight of the cars. There were numerous suitable lakes north of the city, and Brack and his friends would create a road course on the ice by plowing off the snow cover, which was generally just pushed to the side so that the course was lined by snowbanks.

The rules were easy—when the flag dropped, you'd go like hell until you saw the checkered flag!

They ran cars in classes designated by engine displacement, such as under 1000 cc, under 1500 cc, under 2000 cc, over 2000 cc, etc., and most cars back then were rear-wheel driven. There were also classes for studded tires and non-studded tires, and as you can imagine, lots of paint was exchanged, but most of the cars then were just old clunkers, and the racers had hours of fun. Any car that could run was good enough, including British imports Morris Minors, Ford Anglias and Mini Coopers and the big American-made Dodges, Fords and Chevys. Some racers, though, worked for dealerships and had access to superior cars; in fact, Brack, who worked as a salesman at Ensign Motors, was just such a driver and once raced a brand new Jaguar across the ice.

Many of the sports' top drivers, including Indy 500 stars, participated in ice racing throughout the winter and drove their top caliber cars in the summer months. These days, ice racing is organized and sanctioned by CASC (Canadian Automobile Sport Clubs), which imposes a formal set of rules and features well-built Ice Race Specials.

Brack eventually purchased a Mini Cooper from the British car dealership Ensign Motors in Toronto, and as the Minis grew in displacement, he went from rallying and racing the early 850cc to 1000 cc Coopers to the then-ultimate Mini Cooper, the 1275. Bill bought his own dealership, Sports Cars Unlimited, and became the Lotus distributor for Canada. This resulted in his moving to a Lotus 47, a twin cam powered version of the Europa, and from there to a Lotus 47 Formula B, in which he took championships in both 1967 and 1968. He soon graduated to Formula 5000 in a hybrid Lotus. Before long, both the Lotus and BRM teams beckoned, and Brack was given the opportunity to fulfill every driver's ultimate dream: driving in a Formula One race.

In 1968, Team Lotus brought three cars to the St. Jovite race: one for Graham Hill, one for Jackie Oliver and a spare car. At the time, Brack was the Lotus distributor for Canada, and he placed a call to Colin Chapman, mentioning the GP and the possibility of driving the spare car. A deal was struck between the two, and for a sum of $6000, Brack was allowed to drive the spare car. Brack then requested to attend the Toronto press conference with Graham Hill the week prior to the race. When Brack met up with Hill before the press conference, he casually mentioned to Hill how excited he was to drive alongside the star. Hill, apparently unaware of the deal made with Chapman, was stunned and told Brack in no uncertain terms that he would NOT be driving the "spare car" at St. Jovite.

Upon arriving at the track the following week, Brack, who had never driven an F1 car before, was instructed to hit the track for five practice laps and not to do anything to jeopardize the car, in other words—don't crash or mess up! He was then instructed to drive five laps during the qualifying session and keep the car in one piece. Jackie Oliver helped talk the inexperienced Brack around the track, especially going into one particular corner that Brack didn't think he could take. Oliver assured him the car could do it and that once he had forced the car to take that corner, it would be easier next time. Little did Brack realize that he was being used more like a guinea pig than a "guest" driver.

You see, in the late 1960s, the Lotus 49 car had a weakness in the rear drive shaft, which had a tendency to twist. Drivers would feel a vibration and then suddenly the drive shaft would snap, sending cars careening off the track. Brack's car was fine that weekend, as his practice and qualifying drives indicated, but Graham Hill felt that warning vibration in his car. Overnight, the team mechanics secretly switched the car's drive shafts, giving Hill the better chance at completing the race. Hill was in the middle of a championship campaign, and it was imperative he had every advantage on the track, so Brack had to be sacrificed. Once the race started the next day, Brack immediately felt the difference in his car's performance. After passing a few competitors, the vibration kicked in and his day in the F1 spotlight was over.

Thirty years ago, this sort of thing was not unusual: the factory team drivers always got the best cars and equipment simply because they were the ones competing for the World Championship and the Constructors' Championship titles. Today, this discreet swapping of parts and equipment would not happen or even need to. Thanks to the huge budgets teams now have to work with, they can afford entire spare cars and a whole range of spare parts for their drivers for every race.

Bill eventually drove in two more Canadian GPs, the 1969 and 1972 races, both for the BRM team, but he failed to take the podium in either. Phil Lamont, the Canadian Dunlop tire distributor who was also track manager for the Comport race circuit at that time, set up the BRM rides for Brack. The team had a couple of extra cars, and Bill was offered the opportunity to get behind the wheel of an F1 car again. Brack actually finished seventh in the 1969 race, but for some unknown reason, his finish was never recorded. During the '72 race, he went off the track at Moss Corner and wasn't able to restart.

After his brief foray into Formula One, he successfully moved over to the Formula Atlantic series in the mid 1970s, where he won three consecutive Canadian Formula Atlantic Championships(1973, 1974 and 1975).

After securing the Formula Atlantic title for the third time, Brack decided to hang up his helmet and work in a slightly safer environment. He opened a car dealership in downtown Toronto, where he incorporated his racing memorabilia and other F1 collectibles in a unique display in his showroom.

Brack is now enjoying a slightly more relaxed life, occasionally driving historic car races in Laguna Beach, but he devotes much of his energy to the new driving school initiative he launched in 2006, the Bill Brack High Performance Driving Academy, located in Dunnville, Ontario. The instruction is focused on advanced driving and highway strategy, and it offers one-day courses in supercars and single-seaters. Bill is extremely proud of his special student-driver training course that empowers young drivers by teaching them accident prevention, skid control and emergency braking techniques, which will hopefully cut down on the number of highway fatalities of young Canadians.

Chapter Seven

Jackie Stewart

BIRTH DATE: June 19, 1939
BIRTHPLACE: Milton, West Dunbartonshire, Scotland

No other Formula One driver has had such an impact on non-race fans as Jackie Stewart. Throughout the '60s and '70s, his distinct Scots accent was lampooned by just about every comedy show from *Monty Python* to *Saturday Night Live*, and he became well-known in the United States as a commentator of televised racing events.

Sir John (Jackie) Stewart, MBE (Member of the Order of the British Empire) was born in Milton, West Dunbartonshire, Scotland, just as World War II was breaking out in Europe. As a youngster, he worked as an apprentice mechanic in his family's garage and Jaguar dealership. Jackie's father had been a motorcycle racer, and Jackie's brother Jimmy was a racing driver with a growing local reputation, having competed in the 1953 British Grand Prix.

It seemed a natural progression for Jackie to pursue a career in motor racing like his older brother.

But after Jimmy was injured in a crash at Le Mans, Stewart's parents discouraged all future racing endeavors for both of their sons. Jackie decided that guns were a safer option and took up shooting competitions, almost making the UK team for the 1960 Summer Olympics.

But a customer of his family's business offered Jackie a position test driving a number of his cars, and when Stewart rolled onto the track, he impressed everyone in attendance that day. Ken Tyrrell, who was running the Formula Junior team for Cooper, heard about the young Scot's performance and contacted Jimmy Stewart to see if Jackie would be interested in a tryout. Without hesitation, Jackie accepted the invitation, taking over the new Cooper F3 that Bruce McLaren had been testing. Soon Stewart was beating the experienced McLaren's times, and upon hearing this, McLaren returned to the track to put in some quicker laps. But Stewart was still faster, and Tyrrell offered Jackie a permanent spot on the team in 1963. This was the beginning of one of F1's greatest partnerships ever.

Starting out the 1964 season, Jackie drove in Formula Three for Tyrrell, winning his first race at Snetterton Motor Racing Circuit. Tyrrell did not compete in Formula One at that time, so in 1965,

Jackie joined BRM alongside Graham Hill and scored his first championship point at the South African GP. Before the end of the year, Stewart won his first race at Monza.

The next year, Stewart almost won the Indy 500 but mechanical failure took him out with only a few laps to go in the race. His performance, however, earned him the Rookie of the Year title.

Also in 1966, Stewart became a spokesman and leader in the fight for improved safety measures in auto racing. In lap one of the Belgian Grand Prix at Spa-Francorchamps, he found himself trapped in his BRM with fuel leaking all over his body. Any spark could have led to tragedy. The race marshals realized they had no tools to help him, so his team-mate Graham Hill leapt from his own car and pulled him out. Ever since then, a main switch for the car's electronics system and a removable steering wheel have become standard equipment on all race cars. Stewart also understood that the long, slow transportation to a hospital could further endanger lives, so he started bringing his own doctor to races, and the BRM team brought in a medical truck for the benefit of all racers.

While racing for Ken Tyrrell's team during the 1968 and 1969 seasons, Stewart drove Matra chassis. His brilliant winning drive through rain and fog during the 1968 German GP at Nürburgring, where

Stewart won by a margin of four minutes, is considered one of the greatest victories ever.

Stewart became World Champion in 1969 behind the wheel of a Cosworth-powered Matra MS80, and until September 2005, when Fernando Alonso drove a Renault to become champion, Stewart was the only driver to have won the championship driving a French car. In 1970, Matra insisted on using its own V12 engines, even though Tyrrell and Stewart wanted to keep the Cosworth engines and maintain their established connection to Ford Motor Company. Consequently, the team bought a chassis from March Engineering, which Stewart drove with moderate success until Tyrrell was able to build its own car later that season. Still sponsored by the French Elf fuel company, Stewart continued to race in a French racing blue–painted car for many years.

Driving the Tyrrell cars, Stewart won the Formula One World Championship in 1971 and 1973, missing the 1972 season owing to severe stomach problems brought on by ulcers that were the result of his years of constant traveling. But his final competitive year, 1973, was marred by tragedy when his friend and protégé Francois Cevert was killed in a crash during practice at Watkins Glen. Earlier that year, Stewart had decided 1973 would be his last year, and after making the announcement, he retired one race earlier than intended, declining to start in what would have been his 100th GP.

Stewart's 27 Grand Prix wins were not equaled for another 20 years, and in 1997, he returned to Formula One as a team owner in partnership with his son, Paul, and the Ford Motor Company. Unfortunately, their cars were not overly successful until Ford acquired Cosworth in the late '90s and they developed the SF3, which brought some wins to the team. In 2000, the team became known as Jaguar Racing when Ford bought out the partnership. Stewart, though, continued to be a spokesman for safer cars and circuits in Formula One.

Now a much respected, retired elder statesman of F1, Stewart fills his life with business interests and giving back to the sport that gave him so much pleasure, fame and wealth. Stewart founded the Mechanics' Trust, a charity benefiting those in the lower levels of motor racing should they be injured while performing their sometimes hazardous jobs in the pits.

Throughout the late '70s and early '80s, the "Flying Scot," as Stewart was affectionately called, covered NASCAR races and the Indianapolis 500 on American television as well as working as an international TV commentator. He was a riveting interviewer and, in the late 1990s, became locked in a verbal sparring match with Ayrton Senna on the subject of Senna's driving etiquette. The racer had just secured his second championship by driving rival Alain Prost completely off the road, something that Stewart would not have done and could never condone. Senna was so incensed by Stewart's stubborn public admonition that he refused to be interviewed by Stewart ever again.

In 1973, Stewart received Sports Illustrated magazine's Sportsman of the Year award, and was named BBC Television's Sports Personality of The Year. In 1990, he was inducted into the International Motorsports Hall of Fame. Ushering in the new millennium, Stewart stepped down as chairman and chief executive officer of Jaguar Racing and was subsequently elected president of the British Racing Drivers' Club.

In 2001, the Queen knighted Stewart and he became a founding patron of the Scottish Sports Hall of Fame. In 2003, the World Forum on the Future of Sport Shooting Activities presented Sir Jackie Stewart with the Sport Shooting Ambassador Award. The award goes to an outstanding individual whose efforts have promoted shooting sports internationally.

Jackie Stewart has always been a great ambassador for integrity and sportsmanship in racing, and few race car drivers have rivaled the impact he's had on 20th century pop culture with his trademark tartan tam o'shanter cap and broad Scots accent.

Chapter Eight

Emerson Fittipaldi

BIRTH DATE: December 12, 1946
BIRTHPLACE: São Paulo, Brazil
RESIDES: São Paulo, Brazil

Brazil excels in two of the world's greatest sports: soccer and auto racing. The country's World Cup soccer teams have ignited the fiery passions of fans of the "beautiful game," and this excitement has extended to their favorite sons on four wheels, in particular Brazil's first Formula One World Champion, Emerson Fittipaldi.

The charismatic young driver became a two-time champion with Lotus and McLaren but suffered several disappointing seasons in his own car before making the successful move over to the U.S. Indy Car series in the 1980s. He retired from driving Champ cars in the mid-'90s after a devastating injury but has remained active in the sport as team owner and even made a surprise comeback in 2005, racing against old time CART rival Nigel Mansell in the GP Masters event held at Kyalami in South Africa, finishing second behind Mansell.

Born in São Paulo to prominent Brazilian motorsports journalist and radio commentator Wilson Fittipaldi Sr. and his wife Juzy, Emerson was named after American author and philosopher, Ralph Waldo Emerson. Both of his parents had raced production cars shortly after World War II, and Wilson Sr. was also responsible for São Paulo's first *Mil Milhas* race in 1956, which was inspired by the 1949 Italian *Mille Miglia*. With his pedigree, there was no doubt that young Emerson would become a keen motorsports enthusiast from an early age.

As a youngster, Fittipaldi started racing motorbikes but soon moved to karts, and in 1967, along with his brother Wilson Jr., he starting building his own karts. The brothers won just about every race they entered. In his second season in single-seaters, 21-year-old Emerson won the Brazilian Formula Vee title. But in the late '60s, all roads led to the UK, so Fittipaldi packed up and moved to Europe, where it took him only three months to convince legendary racing school owner Jim Russell to sign him up for Russell's F3 team. Emerson had secured several podium finishes, and his first victories in Formula Ford helped seal the deal. Driving a Lotus Formula Three car, Emmo won the Lombank F3 Championship with the smooth, controlled driving style that became his hallmark throughout his career.

Under Russell's mentorship, Fittipaldi continued his winning streak, drawing the attention of Colin Chapman, who was looking for a driver to support Austrian Jochen Rindt in the 1970 F1 season. Fittipaldi made his debut at England's Brands Hatch, driving an old Lotus 49 in which he scored an eighth-place finish. His second race took place in Germany, where he scored his first points by taking fourth place.

Although he went in as Chapman's number three driver, Fittipaldi soon became their number one after Rindt was tragically killed at Monza and John Miles left the team. In the first race after Rindt lost his life, Fittipaldi took the checkered flag for Lotus, a real morale-booster for the team, and then went on to secure the World Championship for his fallen teammate. Fittipaldi was lauded as the hero who saved the devastated Chapman/Lotus team.

He continued on a winning streak, and in 1971, his first full year as Lotus' lead driver, Fittipaldi finished an impressive sixth in the Drivers' Championship, but his season was interrupted by a road accident on his way home from one of the races. While his injuries were not life threatening, they certainly contributed to his lack of form; however, his team was busy experimenting with a new chassis, the Lotus 72, which would change the course of F1 history.

Driving what is arguably the greatest Formula One design of all time, Emmo proved unstoppable. He won 5 of 11 races, easily winning the 1972 F1 Drivers' Championship with the legendary Jackie Stewart some 16 points behind in second place. At age 25, Fittipaldi was the youngest champion in F1 history, a record that stood until 24 year-old Spaniard Fernando Alonso won the championship in 2005.

Fittipaldi started the 1973 season as World Champion and it appeared he might secure the title again in 1973, but after three wins in four attempts with the new Lotus 72D, he struggled in the new 72E that was unveiled midway though the year. This time around, the championship standings were reversed from the previous year, with Stewart beating Emerson by 16 points, but the combination of the 72D and E's points earnings were enough to give Team Lotus the 1973 F1 Manufacturers' Championship.

Colin Chapman, hoping to duplicate his previous "super team" of Hill and Clark, signed Swedish driver, Ronnie Peterson to the team. Fittipaldi seemed unfazed at first by this new addition, winning both the Argentine and Brazilian Grands Prix, but the strain of developing the new car as well as being out-qualified by Peterson took its toll on the usually calm, bushy-side-whiskered Brazilian. He made an uncharacteristic error in judgment in France when trying to pass South African Jody Scheckter, causing a collision that ended the race for both cars. Fittipaldi eventually finished the title chase in second place that year. It was time to move on, and this time, he chose McLaren.

Driving the super-efficient McLaren M23, Fittipaldi scored three victories in 1974 and reached the podium four more times, beating out Clay Regazzoni for his second World Championship. The next year, he scored two victories and four podium finishes but could only manage a second place to Niki Lauda in the championship race. To everyone's shock and amazement, Fittipaldi left McLaren at the height of his success to team up with older brother Wilson in his Copersucar-sponsored Fittipaldi team.

Team Fittipaldi was not a world-class organiza-tion like Lotus or McLaren, and Emmo struggled to maintain his position in the field, even failing to qualify for three races. Despite his poor showing, he remained with the family team for five seasons, only managing a best finish of second place. Frus-trated with his lack of success and the "politics" of F1 racing, Fittipaldi retired in 1980 to his native Brazil. By this time, he was heavily in debt, but thanks to his many contacts, goodwill and hard work, Fittipaldi was able to rebuild his fortune.

After four years of inactivity, the racer's heart still beat loudly, and in 1984, Fittipaldi made a remarkable comeback, this time in the U.S. Indy Car series. The 38-year-old spent his first season driving for two teams before joining Patrick Racing as a replacement for an injured driver. Emmo stayed with the team for five years, notching up six victories and numerous podium finishes. He finished the 1989 season with five wins, placing in the top five in every race he completed, which gave him the CART Championship. Fittipaldi dominated the Indianapolis 500, leading 158 of 200 laps. He won by two laps after a dramatic finish in which he and rival Al Unser, Jr., who were both six laps ahead of Raul Boesel in third place, made tire contact in turn three. Unser's car spun out and hit the outside wall, but Fittipaldi was able to maintain enough control to keep his car moving straight. Despite the wreck, Unser gave Fittipaldi a double thumbs-up sign from the infield as he brought his car through turns three and four on the caution-slowed final lap.

Famed team owner Roger Penske hired Fittipaldi in 1990, and the Brazilian continued to be among the top drivers in CART, winning a race with Penske for six years in a row. In 1993, he scored a second Indianapolis 500 victory after taking the lead from defending F1 World Champion Nigel Mansell on lap 185. The race became well known for Emmo breaking Indy victory lane tradition by drinking a celebratory bottle of orange juice instead of a bottle of milk.

Although he was fast approaching 50, Fittipaldi was still racing Champ cars when an injury at the Michigan International Speedway (MIS) ended his career in 1996. In September 1997, while recovering from his MIS injuries, he was flying his private plane across his orange tree farm when it lost power and plunged 300 feet to the ground. Fittipaldi suffered further serious back injuries from which he eventually recovered, but he never returned to the series as a driver. In 2003, he returned to Champ cars as a team owner and also became active as team principal for the Brazilian A1 GP entry.

Emerson Fittipaldi was inducted in the Motorsports Hall of Fame of America in 2001. His celebrated career, though ending rather sadly, had proven him a driver of great talent and integrity with a smooth, easy-going style. His autobiography, *Flying on the Ground*, offers great insight into the man, his family and his machines.

Fittipaldi was married to Maria Helena from 1970 to 1982, and they had two children together, Juliana and Jayson. He and his second wife Teresa have two daughters, Tatiana and Joanna, and a son, Luca. Tatiana is married to 36-year-old Italian F1 driver Max Papis, and in July 2006, Emerson became a grandpa.

Chapter Nine

Juan-Manuel Fangio

BIRTH DATE: June 24, 1911
BIRTHPLACE: Balcarce, Argentina
DEATH DATE: July 17, 1995

Whether you're a dedicated racing fan or a casual observer of the sport, there's one name that sums up Formula One racing: Fangio!

That name still resonates among fans and sports professionals as the first true legend of F1, and there's rarely a television or newsprint race commentary that does not make at least one reference to this great driver. Unlike current F1 drivers, Fangio started his professional racing career at a rather advanced age and was often the oldest driver in the field. His on-track rivals included some of the best drivers ever to sit behind a wheel, especially his greatest rival, Stirling Moss.

Fangio has been lauded as the best driver in racing history, an honor that has endured over F1's nearly six-decade history, and though many consider Alain Prost, Jim Clark and the late, great Ayrton Senna to be in the same league as Fangio, comparisons are difficult considering all the changes the sport has experienced since Fangio's era.

He pioneered the "four-wheel drift" (a cornering technique in which a driver intentionally breaks traction and forces the car into a controlled slide with all four tires operating at large slip angles) and negotiated treacherous corners in spectacular, yet completely controlled, tire-smoking power slides that thrilled onlookers.

Apart from his unequaled car control, Fangio's astonishing strength and stamina enabled him to master the heavy, hard-to-handle cars throughout the more than three-hour-long endurance tests of those early Grand Prix circuits. He possessed a degree of competitiveness, mental fortitude, intense concentration and raw courage that few drivers today can equal.

Fangio was born on June 24, 1911, in the Argentine frontier town of Balcarce to immigrant parents from the Abruzzi region of Italy. The young mechanic opened his own garage after a brief stint in the armed forces, and he soon started competing in local racing events. During Fangio's early endeavors throughout the 1920s and '30s, rides were hard to come by and the local racers drove an unusual variety of autos. Mechanics tinkered with truck and ambulance engines as well as the grand touring cars of the wealthy landowners who occasionally loaned out their vehicles in the hope of benefiting from side bets. In his first race, Fangio drove a converted Ford taxi (hopefully with the meter off) that had almost completely disintegrated by the time he reached the finish line. As his driving skills improved, he eventually moved into American stock cars, favoring the Chevrolet for its speed and endurance.

These early races were not held at venues like the dirt track ovals of NASCAR or around the more genteel village greens practiced by England's racing elite; Fangio's races consisted of long-distance competitions along the mostly dirt and gravel roads of South America's mountains and flatlands. And the drivers needed more than just a packed lunch. The *Gran Premio del Norte* was one particular race that Fangio entered and won in 1940. It was almost 6000 miles long and ran from Buenos Aires, up through the Andes Mountains to Lima, Peru, then back to Buenos Aires, taking nearly two weeks. All repairs had to be completed by either the driver or co-driver at the end of each daily stage. After his win, Fangio and his Chevrolet became an overnight sensation and the toast of Argentina.

But most of Fangio's early races did not end so successfully, with the checkered flag and champagne corks popping. He persevered, though, supporting himself as a mechanic for other drivers as well as for his own team. As the Argentinean motorsports industry began to impose structure and develop organized racing teams, Fangio successfully drove all makes of American modified stock cars, gaining attention and building quite the fan following. He became the Argentine National Champion in 1940 and 1941, but with the outbreak of World War II, his championship career was halted abruptly.

In 1947, several visiting European drivers intrigued Fangio, in particular Italians Achille Varzi and Luigi Villoresi. The Argentine Automobile Club purchased two Maseratis for their drivers to race against the Italians, and Fangio was given one of them. It proved to be a deciding moment in his racing career.

With the support and sponsorship of the Perón government, Fangio moved to Europe where he could continue building his career and hopefully bring fame and racing honor to Argentina. It took several years to accomplish this feat,though, because many of the established race circuits and roads had been destroyed by bombing and heavy use by Allied armies, and the European auto manufacturers were struggling to rebuild. In 1949, at the age of 37,(an "old man" by racing standards), Fangio finally started to enjoy regular success on the European circuit. He won 6 times in 10 starts, becoming a national hero back home in Argentina.

In 1950, he was invited to join the Alfa Romeo GP team, finishing second in the World Championship that same year after battling teammate Nino Farina for the title. The following season, he scored three wins and finished second three more times to claim the first of his five championships.

Fangio seemed destined to continue his winning streak going into the 1952 season, but at Monza, he suffered his first major accident, breaking his neck and missing the rest of the season.

He had recently switched from the Alfa Romeo team to Maserati and had promised to race at Monza in a non-championship event after competing in a race over in Belfast the day before. But Fangio had missed his connecting flight and was forced to drive all night from Paris through the Alps, arriving at the Monza race circuit only 30 minutes before the start of the race. Because of his late arrival, Fangio was forced to start at the back of the grid, and during the early laps, he made a rare mistake. On the second lap he slid across the track and, because of his fatigue, his reactions were too slow. His car hit a bank and somersaulted in the air. Fangio was thrown out of the cockpit and spent the next few hours fighting for his life.

After months of physiotherapy, and with a now permanently stiff upper torso, Fangio returned to his beloved tracks the following year, finishing the season in second place behind the wheel of a Maserati.

Having been a mechanic himself, Fangio always made it his policy to curry favor with his race crew, and he promised them they would receive 10 percent of his winnings each season. During practice for the Italian Grand Prix, he complained his car was vibrating badly, but on the day of the race the vibration disappeared. What he didn't know was that the crafty mechanics had switched cars in the middle of the night, giving Fangio's vibrating car to his teammate Bonetto and setting Fangio up with a "clean" car.

Fangio was both a strong team player and an inspiring team leader, working closely with his mechanics and often wielding wrenches himself, keeping team morale at a peak throughout each season.

By 1954, Fangio was as big a star in his adopted Italy as in Argentina. He won twice that season for Maserati before making a mid-season switch to Mercedes-Benz, for whom he took the checkered flag four more times to win his second World Championship. Fangio was a sensation driving the superb Mercedes W196 Monoposto as part of a dream team that included Stirling Moss.

By the end of the 1955 season, which was overshadowed by the Le Mans disaster in which 81 spectators were killed, Mercedes had won all the titles and withdrew from racing with nothing left to prove. Fangio won four times that year to clinch a third title; then, in 1956, he switched over to Ferrari, replacing Alberto Ascari, who had been killed in an accident. Fangio won three more races, which gave him his fourth championship.

At the German GP in 1957, Juan-Manuel Fangio delivered one of his most sensational perform-ances, regarded by many as the greatest drive in F1 history. He both loved and was in awe of the treacherous Nurburgring circuit. Driving a some-what underpowered Maserati with equipment that was virtually obsolete at the time, the courageous 46-year-old managed to come from behind and pass the two leading high-powered Ferraris driven by Brits Mike Hawthorn and Peter Collins. Fangio straight-lined through one of the final curves to take the checkered flag from under their noses.

Fangio's prowess behind the wheel had never been put to better use than in this race. While the sleek new Ferraris tore around the track, Fangio toiled behind with a weak rear suspension, opting not to take a full load of fuel and using pit strategy to counter his rivals' speed. Unfortunately, his pit stop was disastrous, leaving him with nearly a min-ute to make up behind the lead pack. But lap after lap, he whittled away at each competitor, finally passing Hawthorn on the final lap to win by four seconds.

Juan-Manuel Fangio drove his last race in 1958 at the French Grand Prix. That race day, his

Maserati was not responding to its driver and was about to be lapped by Fangio's old Nurburgring rival Mike Hawthorn. As a mark of respect for the driver referred to as "the maestro" by his peers, Hawthorn braked, allowing Fangio to cross the line ahead of him. Getting out of his car after finishing fourth in the race, Fangio simply turned to his mechanic saying, "It is finished."

Fangio won 24 of his 51 Grand Prix starts, and his record five World Championships stood for nearly 50 years before German star Michael Schumacher wrote his name in the F1 record books in 2006. Fangio's brilliant track record was achieved by some of the greatest displays of driving skill and courage ever seen, and he did it with style, grace and honor, both on and off the track.

Although short, stocky, balding and nicknamed "El Chueco" (bow-legged) by his fans, Fangio possessed a personal magnetism that made him a figure of adulation around the world. Women found him incredibly attractive, and although he never married, he never lacked female companionship. In February 1958, he became even more of an international celebrity when members of Fidel Castro's revolutionary movement kidnapped him while he was visiting Cuba to help draw attention to their cause. But like everyone else who met him, his captors were charmed by Fangio and released him unharmed and in good humor.

After retiring, he became a representative for Mercedes-Benz, often driving demonstration laps in his former race cars. Fangio was a true gentleman. He was blessed with a sense of fair play, generosity of spirit and humility, personal attributes appreciated and praised by his F1 peers. In 1990, amid great celebration, he was inducted into the International Motorsports Hall of Fame.

Juan Manuel Fangio died in Buenos Aires in 1995 at the age of 84 and was buried in his hometown of Balcarce. His name lives on not only in the history books, but also on the highways and autobahns around the world.

Unveiled at the 2005 Geneva Auto Show, the Pagani Automobili Zonda F is one of the fastest supercars ever made and was named for the great Fangio. Built using Pagani's extensive experience in carbon fiber construction, the Zonda is a world leader with regard to engine fit and finish. Pagani Automobili is among a small group of independent supercar manufacturers that challenge the more established competition, such as Porsche and Ferrari. When the Zonda project began, Fangio consulted and influenced Horacio Pagani on every aspect of the car. Pagani was impressed by the legend's great technical sensibility, and Fangio became a major source of inspiration for Pagani's new car.

HOTTEST DRIVERS

Chapter Ten

David Coulthard

BIRTH DATE: March 27, 1971
BIRTHPLACE: Twynholm, Scotland
RESIDES: Monaco
DRIVES: Red Bull, Car #14

Thirty-five-year-old David Coulthard was born in Twynholm, a small village in southwest Scotland with a population of less than 300. At first glance, you would think Coulthard would be the last person to become a Formula One championship contender, but take a closer look at his background and you may just find the secret formula that helped him reach the heights of auto racing fame and glory.

Surrounded by farmland, Twynholm had a school, a shop with a post office counter and two pubs. But there was also a large shed in the center of the village with impressive red lettering that read "Hayton Coulthard". The freight and trucking company was started by David's grandfather in

1916 and is still in business today, managed by David's older brother Duncan.

This region of Scotland is known as Dumfries and Galloway, and it has been producing world-class racing drivers for many years, including the late Innes Ireland—the first Scot to win a GP—who drove his Lotus into first place at the 1961 U.S. Grand Prix.

Ireland attended the same school that David and his father did years later. And who can forget the legendary Scotsman himself, three-time champion Jackie Stewart who also hails from this part of the country? What better role models could a young man wish for? More recently, another Dumfries native, Allan McNish, entered the F1 arena when it was announced he would drive for Toyota starting in the 2002 season.

A keen karter himself, David's father, Duncan, was delighted when, at 12 years old, David decided he would like to try kart racing with a first race at Larkhall in Strathclyde. David developed into a keen driver and had a successful career in the karts from 1982 through to 1988, graduating to Formula Ford in 1989. Here he drove so well that he won the inaugural McLaren/Autosport Young Driver of the Year title. The prize? His first-ever drive in a Formula One car.

Coulthard, nicknamed "Budgie," tore through the junior categories, even though he missed several races because of a broken leg he received in an accident at Circuit de Spa-Francorchamps in 1990. He came back the following year to win Formula Three races at Zandvoort in the Netherlands and in Macau, China. In 1992, he raced in the Formula 3000 series for Paul Stewart Racing, finishing ninth, and in 1993 he improved to third overall and became a test driver for the Williams team.

He continued in the Formula Three series throughout 1993 as well as test-driving, but tragedy changed his career direction with Ayrton Sennas' death at Imola in 1994. Coulthard was finally able to move to the Williams team as a full-time driver, and though he only competed in eight races that year, he finished an impressive eighth in the season's point standings. He had been promoted to the race team alongside Damon Hill for the Barcelona race and spent much of the season driving the second car. He had to step aside, though, for ex-champion Nigel Mansell on four occasions. Renault wanted a marquee name in the second Williams car, and Mansell, reigning Indy Car champion at the time, fit the bill perfectly. Coulthard had exhibited championship form, but bad luck and several errors saw him take just one podium, a second place at Estoril in Portugal. For the season's last three races, he had to sit out while Mansell took his place, but it was announced that he and not Mansell would race for Williams full-time in 1995.

That season, Coulthard continued alongside Damon Hill, winning his first Grand Prix in Portugal, beating both Michael Schumacher in the Benetton and teammate Hill. He finished an impressive third for the championship with 49 points.

Coulthard switched to McLaren in 1996, where he partnered future champion Mika Häkkinen. This maiden season with McLaren was unremarkable to the point of boring as the Mercedes-powered team struggled to find any sort of speed. The year ended with a second place in Monaco, two podium finishes and seventh place in the Drivers' Championship.

In his second year with McLaren, Coulthard finished the 1997 Drivers' Championship tied with Jean Alesi for third place after Michael Schumacher was disqualified. David had scored two wins and would most likely have added more but for a number of problems, including team orders to allow Häkkinen the win at Jerez.

McLaren took the Constructors' Championship in 1998, but David endured even more problems with pit stop confusion, accidents and the occasional mechanical problem. He managed to win his only race of the season at San Marino. His overall speed, though, enabled him to finish third in the Drivers' Championship with 56 points, behind the battling Schumacher and Häkkinen.

A combination of under-performance and bad luck pushed David back into the 1999 championship's fourth place, with two race wins at the British and Belgium GPs and a total of six podiums as team-mate Häkkinen won the title and McLaren lost the constructor title to Ferrari.

In 2000, Coulthard battled with Schumacher and Häkkinen for the Drivers' Championship but eventually fell out of contention into a disappointing third-place finish, even with wins at the British, Belgium, Monaco and France GPs and 10 podium finishes. He endured another scare in May 2000, when he, his then-fiancée Heidi Wichlinski and a personal trainer narrowly escaped death when their Learjet developed engine problems on the way to Lyon, France, and crashed during an attempted emergency landing. Miraculously, David and Heidi walked away with minor injuries; however, both pilots died when the front of the plane disintegrated upon impact.

Coulthard came back the following year with a championship second place but with half the points amassed by runaway winner Schumacher (123 pts).

During Coulthard's subsequent years (2002–03) at McLaren, teammate Kimi Räikkönen regularly out-drove him. But when FIA introduced the single-lap–qualifying rule, Coulthard seemed to develop racer's "stage fright" when faced with this hot lap and was not able to compete at his earlier level. He openly criticized the qualifying decision, and his position with McLaren came into question when Juan Pablo Montoya was named to the team for the 2005 season. Closing out his McLaren days with a ninth place in the 2004 Championship did not bode well for Coulthard securing a ride the following year.

So after nine seasons with McLaren, Coulthard joined the new Red Bull Cosworth team, where he enjoyed a newfound freedom and put in an impressive season as he racked up 24 championship points. The team had been attracted by Coulthard's maturity and experience, so they teamed him with the inexperienced Christian Klien and Vitantonio Liuzzi. To extend Coulthard's F1 career, his contract with Red Bull was pushed forward into the 2006 season, and with Ferrari engines on board and the design talents of Adrian Newey, who recently joined the team from McLaren, Coulthard's winning days may not be over just yet. He has stated that he wishes to remain with the Red Bull team into the 2007 season, hopefully adding even more victories with them.

Although now living in Monaco, a popular tax-haven for those in the sport, for most of the year, David still visits Twynholm regularly, and at Christmas he often shares a pint with his old school mates in the Masonic Arms pub in Kirkcudbright or in the Star Inn in Twynholm. He also frequently visits his own museum located in Twynholm that houses everything from his earliest karting days, including the plastic karting trophies, qualifying sheets, helmets and anything that may be of interest in the future. Started by David's father in 1999, the private collection was kept in a former sugar store, and over the years, Duncan has taken great pleasure in giving his business colleagues, fans and visitors guided tours of the hundreds of pieces of unique racing history. In 2000, after several months of refurbishment, the museum reopened as the David Coulthard Museum and Pit Stop Diner. Visitors to the Museum are often surprised to see David himself clear the tables and wash dishes for his sister-in-law, who runs the diner.

David also owns homes in London and Switzerland and has recently become a hotelier, owning luxury properties in both Monaco and Great Britain.

Fame and fortune have not changed David, and when given the chance, he still talks about his early racing days with the same enthusiasm any young driver at the start of his career might. Although rumored to be close to retiring, at 35 years old, Coulthard still has many years ahead of him of racing in sports premiere leagues and many opportunities to add to his impressive collection of trophies.

The celebrity status, though, has brought its own set of problems for David, many of which involve matters of the heart. He has suffered attacks in the tabloid press concerning his colorful personal relationships with several beautiful women; however, he vigorously denies the more bizarre claims, stating that the tabloid reports were "out of date and inaccurate." He has been associated with a string of gorgeous women including supermodel Heidi Klum, British aristocrat Lady Victoria Hervey and models Andrea Murray and Ruth Taylor. He has also been engaged to models Heidi Wichlinski and Simone Abdelnour, but in June 2006, the former Belgium racing journalist, Karen Minier, became the new light of his life. Wedding plans are reportedly in the works, following the example set recently by newlywed friend Jacques Villeneuve.

David enjoys an eclectic appreciation of music and lists the Corrs, Queen, Phil Collins, the Cranberries and Oasis as among his current favorites. In the kitchen, he enjoys Italian and Thai cuisine, lots of vegetables, pasta—he has admitted that he will try basically anything edible!

Coulthard remains the highest-scoring British driver in history with 500 points (as of the 2006 Australian GP), easily beating Nigel Mansell's previous record of 482 points. At the 2006 Spanish Grand Prix, he also became the eighth member of Formula One's "200 Club," joining Riccardo Patrese, Michael Schumacher, Rubens Barrichello, Gerhard Berger, Andrea de Cesaris, Nelson Piquet and Jean Alesi in the list of drivers to have competed in 200 Grands Prix.

In the 2006 Monaco Grand Prix, Coulthard scored his first podium finish with Red Bull Racing, his best result with the team to date and the team's first podium finish. Endearing himself to the younger fans, he wore a red cape during the trophy presentation because the team was promoting the soon-to-be-released film *Superman Returns*. He has impressed everyone in the first half of the 2006 season, which practically guarantees him a contract extension through the 2007 season.

However, should that not come to fruition, he certainly won't be bored; there's a rumored publishing deal worth over three million dollars for Coulthard to write his memoirs upon retirement. Or he can make like Elvis and flip burgers at his own diner back home. We'll all be watching the tabloids for that one.

Chapter Eleven

Felipe Massa

BIRTH DATE: April 25, 1981

BIRTHPLACE: São Paulo, Brazil

RESIDES: Monaco

DRIVES: Ferrari, Car # 6

Teammate to über champion Michael Schumacher, the 25-year-old Brazilian-born Felipe Massa is not content to play second fiddle to anybody, and as the 2006 season progresses, he is proving to be a worthy contender to both his teammate and current 2006 points leader Alonso. According to race insiders, Massa is a name that will surely be added to F1 record books in the near future—the kid from São Paulo is HOT!

Massa was always destined for a career in motorsports, beginning his career, as do many pro auto racers, by taking up karting. Between 1990 and 1997 the young Brazilian developed his skills in the various kart events in his homeland, becoming a serious contender for the many championship titles. He also attracted interest from bigger names in the sport, and in 1998, Felipe graduated to the Formula Chevrolet Championship where he won the series title in 1999.

In 2000, he was on the move again, this time to the Formula Renault series were his talents earned him plenty of praise and respect throughout the season, and while he dreamt of F1, he continued to learn and race in challenging conditions, testing himself on every available surface. By 2001, Felipe packed his bags and moved over to the European F3000 series, becoming series champion that same season with six wins out of eight races, plus plenty of fastest-laps times and pole positions.

These dominating performances finally brought Massa to the attention of Peter Sauber, who is well known for his talent-spotting abilities. Felipe was hoping to get a test drive in F1, but when Sauber offered him a full-time drive in 2002, he jumped at the chance. His maiden season was a mixed bag. His driving was called into question several times as he made mistakes that cost his team points, but everyone admired his spirit. Sadly, Sauber didn't appreciate the value of this youthful enthusiasm, and at the end of the season Massa's contract was not renewed.

As a fresh new season opened, Felipe was courting the Jordan team for a full-time drive but the deal failed. However, in February 2003, lightening struck when he signed on with the legendary

Ferrari organization as an official test driver for the Maranello team. Felipe was given an important role to play for Ferrari, focusing mainly on tire testing to ensure that both Schumacher and then-teammate Rubens Barrichello had the best tires for upcoming races. He learned a lot during his year with Ferrari, especially from Michael Schumacher, and upon completion of his test-drive contract, he re-signed with Sauber for a race seat in 2004. His contract also allowed Ferrari to use him if they required him to test.

Massa was keen to show he really did deserve to be in F1 full time, so he set about scoring points on five occasions and securing 12th place in the Drivers' Championship. The highlight of the season for Felipe was leading one lap of his home Grand Prix at Interlagos, the final race of the season.

Massa remained with Sauber in 2005 and was joined by former champion Jacques Villeneuve. Felipe was unaffected by the presence of a former champion as he blitzed Villeneuve in the first half of the season while the Canadian adapted to life with the Swiss team. Although it was a tough season all-round for the Sauber team, Massa accumulated 11 points with a fourth place best at Montreal, Villeneuve's home turf.

Massa was rewarded with a return invitation to Ferrari for a full-time ride in 2006. The young Brazilian had proven himself, and by teaming up alongside Schumacher, he was handed the golden opportunity to learn from the most successful driver of all time.

He started the 2006 season off in fine form, qualifying second at the opening race in Bahrain; however, he seemed to resume his tendency to spin out in silly places and did so in both the practice session and during the race, where he narrowly missed the eventual winner, Fernando Alonso. In the Malaysian GP, Massa managed to claw his way from the back of the grid, where he started in 21st position, to a fifth-place finish, beating Schumacher who started from 14th. But Felipe continued to drive on the wild side at the Australian GP, crashing his Ferrari in the qualifying session and then again at the first corner in the race.

The handsome Massa is single, though he has been dating the gorgeous Brazilian brunette Raffaela Bassi for a few years. When not on the race circuits around the world, they often enjoy theatre and shopping trips together, and it is rumored that wedding bells may be ringing soon for the couple.

Chapter Twelve

Fernando Alonso

BIRTH DATE: July 29, 1981
BIRTHPLACE: Oviedo, Asturias, Spain
RESIDES: Oxford, England
DRIVES: Renault, Car #1

Fernando Alonso's success has electrified Spain. The 25-year-old was recently awarded the country's highest honor for a sportsman, the title of Prince of Asturias, a cross between the UK's BBC Sports Personality of the Year and the Legion d'Honneur. Crown Prince Felipe may be heir to the Spanish throne, but it is "the prince of F1" that King Juan Carlos calls after each of the young driver's track victories to encourage him and boast of familial pride.

Fernando Alonso's 2005 World Championship also rescued F1 from the five-year dominance of Michael Schumacher and Ferrari. The Spaniard captured his third straight win at the San Marino GP by holding off Schumacher in a thrilling wheel-to-wheel duel over the final 12 laps. That victory was hailed as the greatest race in more than a decade.

Fernando was born on July 29, 1981, in Oviedo in the Asturias province of northern Spain. His mother was a store clerk and his father, José Luis, was an explosives expert in the local mining industry. Although the Alonso's were not a wealthy family, Fernando and elder sister Lorena lived comfortably. José Luis loved kart racing on weekends, and Fernando picked up his father's passion for speed. When the elder Alonso constructed a kart in the image of a miniature F1 car for a somewhat disinterested Lorena, it was three-year-old Fernando who jumped in and took the wheel. From the moment Fernando climbed aboard, he immediately felt at home.

With his father onboard as mechanic, Fernando traveled around the country competing in the numerous karting events. Although he had the support of his devoted family, it was an expensive "hobby" that, if it were to grow into anything more substantial, would require funding that his parents could not handle on their own.

It was difficult to acquire sponsorships—especially for a youngster, no matter how promising a career he seemed to have—and Fernando knew the only way to get the financial backing was to win, win and win some more. And win he did. Alonso won almost every race he entered, invariably as the youngest racer on the track. But his age was never a handicap. He easily won three Spanish Karting titles in 1994, 1996 and 1997; he also raced in the European Kart Championship, scoring a superb second place, and by 1996, he was the World Junior Karting Champion.

Then in 1999, with support from former Minardi Formula One driver Adrian Campos, Fernando graduated to open-wheel racing, competing for Nissan in the Spanish Euro Open.

This was Alonso's first and last season in the series, and at 18 years old, he became the series champion. His first Nissan Fortuna test came at Albacete, and this was, surprisingly, the first time he had ever driven a car with a clutch and gear-box. The test lasted a mere 20 minutes because of a guardrail scrape, but Fernando had already equaled the lap record.

The drive immediately earned him a ticket to Formula 3000 in the 2000 season. A win at the legendary Spa-Francorchamps circuit led to a solid fourth-place finish in the Drivers' Championship, and Alonso was once again on the move in 2001, this time over to the big show: Formula One.

Under the management of Flavio Briatore, then Benetton's F1 boss, Alonso was signed to the Anglo-Italian team as test driver. In a surprise move, he was loaned out to Minardi, with whom he made his F1 debut on March 4 in Melbourne, Australia, becoming the third youngest driver ever to start an F1 Grand Prix.

Although he was driving an extremely under-performing car, Alonso was sensational, out-qualifying many of his more well-known rivals. But, because the TV directors only focused on the front-runners, much of Fernando's brilliant driving went unnoticed. He raced out the season with no wins and failed to score any competition points, but he had started to build his reputation as a tenacious competitor on the track. The TV cameras were now starting to point in his direction.

In 2002, Fernando returned to Benetton, which was now owned by Renault. His driving talents earned him a spot as a test driver with the newly founded team run by Briatore. Fernando was groomed to become a regular driver for the following season. He was given a much more powerful and better-equipped car to drive, and he soon stunned race fans when, at the 2003 Malaysian GP, he became the youngest driver ever to win an F1 pole. It came as no surprise when it was announced in mid-summer that Alonso would replace British driver Jenson Button in 2003.

Fernando was the sensation of 2003, finishing third in Malaysia and Brazil, followed by a convincing second in the Spanish GP. Then, at the 2003 Hungarian Grand prix, he became the youngest driver ever to win a Formula One race. By season's end, he was a solid sixth in the championship, with 55 points and four podium finishes.

Despite his bravery and ability, Alonso still had much to learn. In particular, he needed to curb his tendency to over-drive his car; his 2003 accident at Interlagos was preventable and was not helped by his fiery Latin temperament. However, Alonso has proven that he is one of the few drivers capable of being on pace in every lap of every race, and he has the rare ability of driving around major problems while losing minimal lap time.

Alonso remained with Renault throughout the 2004 season, but the difficult-to-drive R24 kept him out of victory lane. The season started well enough with a third place in Australia, but he then had to wait until mid-season, at Magny Cours, to gain his second podium position. Back-to-back podiums followed in Hockenheim and Hungary. In the early part of the year, though, team management had been questioning their decision to retain Alonso because he was constantly being out-qualified and out-raced by teammate Jarno Trulli. Fortunately, his performance turned around toward the end of the year. This was about the same time that Trulli suffered a mysterious lack of form after dropping Renault boss Flavio Briatore as his manager. Trulli's relationship with the team deteriorated, resulting in him signing with Toyota from 2005 onwards; he actually left to join his new team three races from the close of the 2004 season. Alonso may have had no wins under his belt, but he ended the year with a career-best fourth in the championship standings, scoring 59 points and four podiums. He was also able to outpace his new teammate, the 1997 World Champion, Jacques Villeneuve, who replaced Jarno Trulli for those final three races of the season.

Then came 2005, a watershed year for Alonso, in which he recorded seven race wins. The young Spaniard made the best of his ultra-competitive R25 package, beating season-long rival Kimi Räikkönen to the title by 21 points. He also delivered Renault their first Constructors' Championship with the help of new teammate, Giancarlo Fisichella.

Fernando finished third in the first race of the season in Australia. In the second race in Malaysia he nailed the pole position during qualifying and easily won the race. He repeated this feat in the next race, winning the Bahrain GP from the pole position, and continued his good form with a close win over Michael Schumacher in the San Marino Grand Prix after a 13-lap battle with the seven-time world champion. Schumacher constantly maneuvered his Ferrari around the track, trying to set up a pass, but Alonso blocked him each time. Schumacher got half his car alongside Alonso on the final lap, but Alonso would not budge. It was a duel the likes of which F1 hadn't seen since Ayrton Senna and Nigel Mansell went wheel-to-wheel at Monaco back in 1992.

While he did not win the Spanish Grand Prix, Alonso drove consistently to finish second behind Kimi Räikkönen, who again trumped Alonso at Monaco where the Spaniard suffered severe tire wear. Alonso did, however, manage to take fourth place. Räikkönen delivered one of the most memorable moments of the 2005 season with a spectacular exit from the European Grand Prix at the Nürburgring, giving the win to Alonso. But Alonso's run of good luck came to an abrupt end at the Canadian Grand Prix when he made a serious mistake after coming under pressure from Juan Pablo Montoya and Räikkönen, both driving McLarens. He crashed into the wall at the Villeneuve corner, damaging his suspension, and was forced to retire—his first race retirement of the year.

In the U.S. GP, only six of the 20 cars competed. Alonso and the other Michelin drivers refused to start because Michelin informed them their tires would not be safe to use on the newly resurfaced track. On race day, thousands of spectators in the stands stood and booed as only the teams using Bridgestone tires took the starting grid. The event sullied F1's image, especially in the U.S., where the sport had been trying to establish itself for 20 years.

The French GP was the site of Alonso's third pole position of the season, and he again led the race from start to finish, resulting in his fifth triumph of the year. He followed this with another pole the following week at the British GP, this time finishing second behind a McLaren-Mercedes driven by Colombian Juan Pablo Montoya, who took his first victory of 2005.

But McLaren's poor reliability opened the door for Alonso's next win at the German GP when Kimi Räikkönen's car suffered a hydraulic failure.

Two days before the Hungarian GP, Alonso celebrated his 24th birthday. Unfortunately, he did not get the birthday gift he had hoped for: he qualified a disappointing sixth and finished out of the points at 11th place after a collision with Ralf Schumacher.

Alonso continued his steady march toward the championship with podiums at the Turkish Grand Prix, Monza and the Belgian Grand Prix. He finally caught a break when he qualified on pole for the Brazilian GP, where he finished third, clinching the Drivers' Championship title at the age of 24 years and 59 days old, breaking Emerson Fittipaldi's long-standing record of being the youngest F1 champion in history by some 18 months. His win also ended the five-year dominance of über-racer Michael Schumacher. In fact, Alonso had led the championship standings from the second race of the season.

Alonso's win at the Chinese GP gave Renault their first Constructors' Championship.

Thanks to Fernando's success as the country's first Formula One World Champion, Spain has been gripped by "Alonsomania." Alonso hails from the heart of the same working-class area that gave birth 13 centuries ago to the Christian "Reconquista" that resulted in the expulsion of the Moors who had ruled most of Spain for 800 years. On his helmet, Alonso wears the region's yellow cross, which Pelayo used when he defeated the Moors around A.D. 718 in Asturias. Legions of Alonso fans follow their hero from one race to another across the globe, waving their light blue Asturian flags with the yellow cross.

But there was a shock to come for both his fans and racing insiders at the end of his championship season: Alonso announced that he would be leaving Renault and joining arch-rivals Vodafone McLaren Mercedes for the 2007 season. This announcement prompted immediate speculation regarding Renault's F1 future. To end off his final season with Renault, Alonso won his second consecutive world title at the Grand Prix in Brazil.

To escape intrusive media scrutiny, Alonso lives quietly in a riverside apartment in Oxford, England, just a short drive from the Renault team's headquarters in Enstone. He is an intensely private man who speaks quietly and comes across as shy and modest off the track. His girlfriend, Carolina, stays away from races to avoid celebrity photographers. Very little is known of her background or how they met. Alonso is very connected with his family, but fame prevents him from going home to Oviedo because there would be at least a thousand people waiting in front of his family home. He occasionally catches a soccer game at Real Madrid but has to don a disguise and enter the stadium after the game has already started.

Even the start of the 2005 all-Spanish tennis final in Barcelona between Rafael Nadal and Juan Carlos Ferrero was delayed 15 minutes because fans were too interested in Alonso's latest victory to focus on the tennis match! Before Alonso's charge toward the F1 Championship, Spain had no significant television deal in place to broadcast F1 races, but now nearly five million Spanish fans tune in to watch each race, delivering far more television viewers than the UK or France.

It is well known that mainstream media, especially the British tabloids, have a reputation for building up a person, whether it's an actor, musician or sports star, then taking great pleasure in knocking them down. And there were times, especially toward the end of the 2005 season, when it seemed as though they all had Fernando Alonso in their sights.

Alonso had driven superbly throughout the season, but it appeared that the media, as well as many race fans, regarded him as the villain of the piece. They were all cheering for Kimi Räikkönen. In fact, at the end of the year it was the hot young Finn who was voted Driver of the Year, but Alonso's achievements leave no margin for doubt—he deserved all the laurels. He was the champion and will always own that title.

Chapter Thirteen

Giancarlo Fisichella

BIRTH DATE: January 14, 1973
BIRTHPLACE: Rome, Italy
RESIDES: Rome, Italy
DRIVES: Renault, Car #2

Whether he's wearing his safety helmet or not, there's no mistaking the deep brown eyes and finely chiseled jaw line of Giancarlo Fisichella.

The 33-year-old son of Rome, also known as "Fisico" or "Fisi" to fans and friends, began kart racing as a youngster. In 1991, he graduated to his first car racing team, Formula Alfa Boxer, then competed for three seasons in the Italian F3 series, racing for RC Motorsport. He was runner-up in the 1993 championship but clinched the title the following year, the same year he won the Monaco F3 race, as well as one of the two heats of the International Invitation race at Macau. He left open-wheel racing briefly in 1995, driving for Alfa Romeo in the International Touring Car Championship series but soon returned to his first love, making his Formula One debut in 1996 with the Minardi team. He remained with Minardi until he was replaced by Giovanni Lavaggi.

With a move over to Jordan racing in 1997, Giancarlo thrived, taking a second place podium finish in the Belgian Grand Prix and leading the German Grand Prix before retiring with mechanical problems. Fisi had been tapped early on to become the successor to greats such as Prost, Senna and Stewart, and that year he also outclassed reigning Formula Nippon champion Ralf Schumacher, his teammate. At Hockenheim, he led for much of the race but was denied the win by an inspired Gerhard Berger and a puncture. A superb second behind Schumacher at Spa in drenching conditions marked him as a real talent. After a successful 1997 season when he finished in eighth place overall, he moved to the Benetton team for the 1998 season, achieving the first pole position of his career as well as two second place finishes, ending the season ninth overall, with 16 points.

Benetton was not running competitive cars— they were without the Renault works engines—and the 1999 season didn't turn out the way Fisi had hoped. Although he achieved a few podium place wins, his car was inconsistent. At the Nurburgring, Fisichella had been leading and was on course for the much-needed win, but he crashed out. This was his last chance for a win for several years. Finishing the season in ninth place again, this time with only 13 points, he hoped for a turn-around in 2000 but couldn't come through.

Podiums early in the 2000 season gave him reason to feel confident; however, Benetton's poor second half of the season meant that Fisi failed to score any more points. Since joining the team, Giancarlo had outclassed teammate Alex Wurz, who made way for up-and-coming star Jenson Button in 2001.

By 2001, Renault owned the team, but that season's car was still performing poorly. They experimented with wide-angle engines that did not deliver competitive levels of power, so for the better part of the year, the Benetton drivers were left to scrap with the Minardis. However, their efforts delivered some improvements. At Hockenheim, Fisichella led home a 4–5 finish, then at Spa he put in a heroic drive to grab the team's only podium of the year. Despite his dominance over teammate Button that year, he found himself forced out to make room for Jarno Trulli in 2002. Fisi returned to Jordan but the team was in decline.

He started 2002 alongside Japanese rising star, Takuma Sato but again, it wasn't the season he was hoping for. As the Japanese GP drew to a close in October, Giancarlo had only a meager seven points to his name, thanks to three fifth-place and one sixth-place finish. With Jordan's new Ford-powered engines behind his new EJ13 ride, Fisi looked forward to a much better 2003.

But again, Lady Luck frowned down on Fisi with an uncompetitive car. In the midst of freak weather conditions, Giancarlo took his first victory at a wet Brazilian GP under a shadow of controversy. He had battled McLaren's Kimi Räikkönen amidst the heavy rain and countless crashes before taking the race lead on lap 53, just before the race was red-flagged. But he was demoted to second place on the podium, because it was presumed that Räikkönen was the race leader two laps prior to the red flag. Several days later, however, the FIA determined that Fisi-chella had already begun his 55th lap prior to the red flag, which meant that he and not Räikkönen had been leading the race two laps before its prema-ture end. Finally, Fisi was awarded his very first F1 victory.

He followed that with a seventh place at India-napolis, which modestly enhanced his score. But Fisi had apparently lost his motivation and felt a fresh new challenge awaited him in 2004 over at the Sauber team.

Home life for Fisichella was looking brighter, though, with a beautiful fiancée, Luna, and their two children, Carlotta and Christopher. Fisi has also become active in a number of children's charities and often lends his name and presence to international fundraisers.

Fisichella's new start with Sauber was seen as a springboard to Ferrari, every driver's dream team. Fisi drove well all season, comfortably outpacing Massa for much of 2004 and finishing with an 11th place championship standing. Strong performances brought him back to the notice of old Benetton team boss Briatore, and by the end of the year, another new two-year deal was in place for 2005 with the Anglo-French outfit.

So Giancarlo returned to Benetton, which by this time had been purchsed by Renault. A pole and win at Melbourne signaled his Formula One breakthrough, but sadly for him, that was the high point in a tough season. More bad luck ruined many of his outings and teammate Fernando Alonso began to dominate. Fisichella often found himself in a strong position only to have something go wrong at the end. Many in the media hinted that the technical problems hampering Fisi's season were a result of team resources being directed at teammate and World Championship leader Fernando Alonso. Alonso went on to claim the championship, and Renault secured the Constructors' title, but Fisichella only reached the podium twice following his Melbourne win. Many felt that Fisichella did not capitalize on his chances. He surrendered on the last lap to Kimi Räikkönen at Suzuka, which cost him the win and prompted many to question his mindset.

But on November 21, 2005, Fisichella's mind was set on a speedy run when he had his road license confiscated for traveling 148 km/h in a 60 km/h zone on the outskirts of Rome. He later confirmed that he was rushing to his son's hospital bed. His boy eventually recovered; however, Fisi's driving career needed a big boost to recover his standing in championship points and retain a driving seat for 2006.

The new year started off as usual with a great performance when he won in Malaysia, thanks in part to Alonso's fuel rig glitch (his crew over-loaded the car with fuel, resulting in a penalty). But Fisi could not shake off the jinx that rode with him. At both Imola and Nürburgring, Giancarlo missed the top 10 in qualifying, later blaming Jacques Villeneuve for blocking him during one of his qualifying laps at Nürburgring.

Giancarlo Fisichella is considered one of Formula One's fastest drivers, but after so many seasons with poorly performing cars, his motivation may have suffered, and it has been suggested that his problems are more mental than mechanical. Every driver needs strong support from his team to perform to his maximum ability, and his fans, who are just as frustrated as he is with the lack of wins, are keeping fingers crossed that by the end of 2006, the name Fisichella will be engraved on the championship trophy.

Chapter Fourteen

Jacques Villeneuve

BIRTH DATE: April 9, 1971
BIRTHPLACE: St-Jean-sur-Richelieu, Quebec, Canada
RESIDES: Villars-sur-Ollon, Switzerland
DRIVES: BMW Sauber, Car # 13

Just 24 when he became the youngest-ever Indy 500 winner and CART champion, Jacques Villeneuve took only two years to become the F1 World Champion. He was among the first group inducted into Canada's *Walk of Fame* and was also named Canada's Athlete of the Year in both 1995 and 1997. In 1998, he was made an Officer of the National Order of Quebec.

The multi-tasking Canuck has also ventured into the movies with a small cameo as (surprise!) a race car driver in Sylvester Stallone's 2001 action film *Driven*, and he owns one of Montreal's hottest nightclub and restaurant properties, called *Newtown* after the English translation of his last name (*ville* is French for *town*, and *neuve* means *new*). In 2006, he announced he was entering the recording industry with a new 13-track folk/rock CD to which his on-track rival, Michael Schumacher, responded with a sarcastic comment to the media, "Maybe that's where he can be competitive."

Schumacher isn't the only one who has had doubts about the 35-year-old racer, whose career has fluctuated from championship to numerous DNF's, but with his new wife, Johanna, and a baby on the way, Villeneuve has an almost Zen-like attitude to match his new-found maturity and is not fazed by the fact he hasn't won a race since 1997 or been on the podium since 2001. Life is good, and the wins will come. His fans, though, are hoping those wins arrive sooner than later!

Jacques Joseph Charles Villeneuve was born on April 9, 1971, in the Quebec town of St. Jean-sur-Richelieu. His father was legendary F1 driver Gilles Villeneuve, and his uncle, for whom he was named, was a relatively successful driver on the U.S. and Canadian road racing circuits. With such a pedigree, it was no wonder that young Jacques entered the family business, competing for three years in the Italian Formula Three series starting in 1989. In 1997, he became one of only three drivers ever to win the Indianapolis 500, the Champ Car Championship and the Formula One World Championship (Emerson Fittipaldi and Mario Andretti were the other two).

Jacques' famous father died when the youngster was just 11 years old, so he had little hands-on influence over his son's career. In 1986, Jacques' mother, Joann, allowed her son to follow the family tradition, and under the guidance of his uncle, the teenager signed up for an intense course of training under the tutelage of Jim Russell at his driving school in Mount-Tremblant, Quebec. Jacques' first classes were behind the wheel of a modified Ford, adapted to fit his then-small frame. During his first efforts on the track, it became apparent that he had inherited his father's natural talent and hunger for speed.

Between 1987 and 1991, Jacques raced in North American and Europe, sharpening his skills while taking podiums in Canada and Italy and moving into Formula Three. He ranked sixth overall despite not winning a single race. Villeneuve then moved to the Japanese Formula Three in 1992, finishing runner-up after winning three times. During this period, he made an important decision that would impact his career. Villeneuve asked Craig Pollock, his ex-professor of physical education at the Beau Sun College in Switzerland, to become his manager.

The stars seemed to align perfectly for Jacques after he joined the Forsythe-Green team and moved over to the North American Toyota Atlantic series, where he won five times on tracks that he had never seen before. He moved swiftly to Champ Car racing and was crowned Rookie of the Year in 1994 after a string of strong results, including his first victory at Elkhart Lake, Wisconsin. That same year he scored a second place in the Indianapolis 500 and a win at Road America for the Forsythe team, ranking sixth overall for the season. The 1995 season brought even more accolades when Jacques took the Indy Championship title as well as winning the famed Indianapolis 500, where he actually drove 505 miles because of a two-lap penalty. Villeneuve became the last Indycar Champion prior to the 1996 controversial division of the CART and IRL series, which left fans and media confused and angry. At the time of writing, however, the two race organizations appear to have come to a business agreement and should be merging back into a single entity.

During the summer of 1995, Villeneuve participated in several tests for the Williams F1 racing team, and within a matter of weeks it became clear to one and all that Jacques would emulate his father by shifting gears and changing lanes to the world of F1. And he certainly entered F1 with a bang, securing the pole position in his first Grand Prix at Melbourne, assuring one and all that he could make the transition from CART to F1 like no one before him. It only took four races before he won his first F1 race at Nurburgring.

Jacques scored three more Grand Prix wins in 1996 and managed to push teammate Damon Hill all the way to the final race of the year in Japan with Hill finally triumphant...just!

Within a year, Villeneuve became the undisputed star of the Williams team and soon embarked on a rivalry of mythic proportions with Michael Schumacher for the World Championship. A controversial collision with Ferrari's gifted but volatile driver at Jerez gave Jacques the 1997 World Championship, but he encountered serious difficulties trying to defend his title the following season. Renault had left F1, leaving the Williams team at a technical and mechanical disadvantage to McLaren and Ferrari, so Villeneuve packed his bags at the start of the new racing calendar and rejoined his former Indy car boss, Craig Pollock, at the start of a brand new F1 venture, British American Racing(BAR).

The 1999 season was difficult for both team and driver as they struggled with equipment reliability, but the ongoing development paid off big time in 2000 when Jacques started amassing championship points to end the season in seventh place. The following year started badly with a huge wreck at the Melbourne GP that resulted in the tragic death of a race marshal, and the team was not convinced their driver was doing his best; however, thanks to some long-awaited strong performances, Jacques delivered BAR's first podium finishes in Spain and Germany.

At the end of 2001, a major management reorganization at BAR resulted in Villeneuve's friend and manager Pollock being released from his contract. He was replaced by Prodrive boss David Richards, with whom Villeneuve felt less than comfortable, and Jacques struggled to maintain his prior form throughout the 2002 season. With only one year left on his contract, Villeneuve turned down a lucrative opportunity to race in CART before returning to BAR for 2004 and 2005. Instead he chose to fulfill his original deal in the hope of landing a ride with another Grand Prix team the following year. But he and Richards clashed publicly over salary, and his track performance suffered. In 2003, Villeneuve was roundly criticized by the media for being regularly outpaced by his younger, less experienced teammate, British hunk Jenson Button. Jacques launched a string of verbal attacks against Button, who he dismissed as a lightweight, but as the season progressed, Button raced extremely competitively, and Villeneuve changed his attitude. It was too little too late for the media. Villeneuve's reported $19 million annual salary was also questioned, especially because he scored only six championship points that year.

No longer the "golden boy," Villeneuve had few options on the horizon for 2004. When BAR suddenly announced that Takuma Sato would replace him behind the wheel next season, he quit one race early, and Sato quickly filled in for the temperamental Canadian at the Japanese GP. BAR eventually would go from fifth to second place in the Constructors' Championship following Ville-neuve's departure.

He started 2004 without a drive, but Renault came calling for the final three races of the season, offering him a ride to replace the increasingly under-performing Jarno Trulli. Villeneuve finally received the call he was waiting for: an offer to drive with Sauber Petronas for 2005 alongside Felipe Massa.

With a two-year contract in hand, Villeneuve got his season with Sauber off to a disappointing start, and by the time the team went to San Marino, rumors circulated that he was going to be dropped. Villeneuve picked up his pace as the sea-son progressed, and the rumors eventually died down, especially after his sixth-place finish at the Belgian Grand Prix. Team owner Peter Sauber decided to sell his team to BMW. They planned to run the team under the name BMW Sauber in 2006, and to Villeneuve's relief, his name was on the 2006 team roster.

He started the 2006 calendar by blowing an engine in the opening race but finished a promis-ing seventh in his second race, which delivered

BMW's first points of the season. He gained further championship points in Australia with a sixth-place finish after starting 19th because of an engine change. Then, on home turf at the 2006 Montreal Grand Prix, he wrecked and was unable to finish.

On August 1, 2006, BMW team chief Mario Theissen announced that Jacques would be replaced in the BMW-Sauber car at the Hungarian Grand Prix by Polish driver Robert Kubica, who became the first Polish driver to contest a Formula One race. After his recent crash at Hockenheim, Jacques had indicated he was not ready to drive again. Kubica was a test driver for the team and now that he has been moved into a full-time seat, Villeneuve's future is uncertain at time of this writing. But it is certain that he will no longer be with the BMW-Sauber team.

But life for Jacques is not all racing. He enjoys computer games, alpine skiing, rollerblading and hockey and is an avid reader, favoring history and science fiction books. He also loves music, in particular rock and pop, and is an accomplished pianist and guitar player. As a child, he even learned the trumpet. Traveling around the world for a living, he now speaks Italian as well as English and his native French, so he is able to order his favorite food, pasta, wherever he goes. Jacques has remained close to his family, which includes his mother, Joann, his sister, Melanie, and his half-sister, Jessica.

Although Villeneuve has retained his Canadian citizenship, he resides in Villars-sur-Ollon, Switzerland, and maintains a home in Monaco. He was once engaged to Sandrine Gros D'Aillon(a college student from Montreal), Australian singer Dannii Minogue (superstar Kylie's sister) in the late 1990s and American ballerina Ellie Green. In 2006, he married his Parisian girlfriend, Johanna Martinez, in two separate ceremonies. Jacques and his 21-year-old bride exchanged vows in a civil ceremony in Switzerland at the 12th-century fortress of Chateau d'Aigle. A day after Jacques raced in the Monaco GP, friends and family joined the couple in a Paris church for the religious nuptials. After the wedding, the bride and groom dined with their guests in the resort town in the Alps where Jacques lives, and the Canadian press has reported the happy couple is also expecting their first child.

Chapter Fifteen

Jarno Trulli

BIRTH DATE: July 13, 1974
BIRTHPLACE: Pescara, Abruzzo, Italy
RESIDES: St. Moritz, Switzerland
DRIVES: Toyota F1, Car #8

Born in Pescara, Italy in 1974, Jarno was named after Jarno Saarinen, the Finnish Grand Prix motorcycle racing champion, who was killed at Monza in 1973. When he first entered F1, Jarno's Finnish name caused some confusion with the Italian media who did not realize that he was indeed Italian.

His father's enthusiasm prompted Jarno's early entry in to karting at age three, where he developed his driving and analytical skills for 12 years. He has stated that it was important for him to get his grounding in karting, and he racked up an impressive list of achievements prior to his debut in Formula One: he is the only F1 driver to have won everything there is to win in karting from numerous World and Italian kart titles, the 1987 Youth

Games Gold Medal, and the US, Japanese and Hong Kong Kart CP Championships. Midway through 1995, Flavio Briatore, the suitably impressed Benetton boss, paid for Trulli to enter into German Formula Three, where he won the remaining two races of the season for the KMS team.

Jarno won the German F3 Championship in 1996; then in 1997, thanks to Briatore stepping in once again, he made his debut in Formula One with the Minardi team, replacing Tarso Marques. Racing in Australia, he finished a respectable ninth after starting back in the grid at 17th position. But as the season played out, he was continually hampered by mechanical failure and lack of power. When Marques returned for the French GP, Jarno moved over to the Prost team after its driver, Olivier Panis, was injured at Montreal. He finished fourth in the German Grand Prix, amazing everyone by leading for more than half the race at Austria before his engine blew. He signed for Prost full-time in 1998 with his best finish—6th place—coming at Belgium.

Jarno stayed with the Prost team for the next two seasons and eventually scored his first podium at the 1999 European GP. But 1999 saw Jarno handicapped by unreliable engines, which stopped him from proving his talent and passion, although toward the end of the season he had some fairly strong qualifying performances, including a second-place finish in Nurburgring, his first F1 podium.

Sensing Jarno's concern for his future, Eddie Jordan quickly signed the young Italian to replace the retiring Damon Hill to partner Heinz-Harald Frentzen for the coming 2000 season. Trulli delivered some strong drives; he was the only other driver not in a McLaren or a Ferrari to take a front row grid position throughout the entire year. However, because of on-track incidents involving other drivers or engine inconsistency problems with the EJ10, Jarno just couldn't turn his strong starts into podium finishes.

And 2001 was even worse, producing a season filled with constant failures despite strong qualifying performances. Jarno hoped that by switching places with Giancarlo Fisichella at Renault for 2002, he would finally get to show what he was made of. He eventually finished the season with nine championship points overall, five points behind teammate Jenson Button, thanks to a couple of fourth-place finishes in Monaco and Italy.

Button left the team in 2003, replaced by up and coming star Fernando Alonso.

Despite finishing eighth in that year's championship and being overshadowed by Alonso, the future championship contender, Jarno Trulli started 2004 in fine style, excelling from the Australian to the French GPs. But in the second part of his season from Silverstone on to Monza, Trulli's driving proved a disaster, he was unceremoniously dismissed from the team.

Renault made it clear at the season mid-point that Trulli would not be with the team in 2005. His relationship with former manager and team boss Flavio Briatore deteriorated, regardless of a redeeming Pole position at Spa-Francorchamps. Following the Italian GP, Trulli was released from his contract and joined Toyota for the last two races of 2004. Despite all the turmoil, Trulli managed a sixth-place finish in the championship.

For his first full season with Toyota, Trulli made the best of his new chance, driving full on at the start of the 2005 season, claiming three podium positions in the first five races. But his track record of lousy seasonal second halves haunted him with a disappointing finish to the year. His TF105 was an impressive package, and Trulli's supreme qualifying efforts helped Toyota move into fourth place in the Constructors' Championship. He also achieved Toyota's first pole position at the ill-fated U.S. GP race. Until the final few races of the season, Trulli seemed set for a good showing in the championship, but he finally lost out to teammate Ralf Schumacher as the pair took sixth and seventh positions.

As the 2006 season plays out, Trulli finds himself in much the same position in the championship points standing, and he is attempting to move

Toyota further up the Constructors' title ladder to the top of the podium.

Jarno had never dreamt of becoming an F1 driver; he would have been happy remaining in karting. It wasn't until he won the F3 championship in 1996 that he began to think about a potential career in Formula One. He has been quoted as saying he doesn't want or need to be famous; he just wants to be a good, winning driver. Although the top spot on the podium has eluded him to date, many insiders predict it's just a matter of time before Jarno Trulli's name is engraved on a big trophy.

In the meantime, he has the loving support of wife Barbara who delivered their first child, a son, in 2005. Continuing in the family tradition, Jarno named his boy after one of his heroes, his dad Enzo. The family resides in St. Moritz, Switzerland, for most of the year, where Jarno keeps in shape when not on the track by swimming, playing tennis, cycling and getting in lots of gym time.

With his international lifestyle, Jarno Trulli admits he is not a "typical Italian." He arrives early for appointments, displays a calm and understated personality and doesn't even care about soccer. In fact, he completely overlooked Italy's recent triumph at the 2006 World Cup.

But one thing no one can overlook is Trulli's talent and passion for F1. Whether he likes it or not, he will be famous one day soon.

Chapter Sixteen

Jenson Button

DATE OF BIRTH: January 19, 1980
BIRTHPLACE: Frome, Somerset, England
RESIDES: Monaco
DRIVES: Honda Racing F1, Car #12

British heartthrob F1 racer Jenson Button is, in the words of Austin Powers, a real "cheeky monkey." Starting out as a "media darling," he was once considered the David Beckham of F1, being referred to as a clotheshorse, author (he started writing his own autobiography at age 19!), TV personality and playboy with a singer/TV star girlfriend. However, since the early part of the 2005 season, he has not lived up to the promise with numerous contract disputes, poor race results and high-profile personal meltdowns that contributed to his fall from grace with sports media. But that million-dollar smile and his movie-star good looks keep his female fans loyal and race cameras on him.

Born Jenson Alexander Lyons Button in Frome, England, on January 19, 1980, Jenson is the son of former '70s British rally-cross star John Button, who named his son for his favorite car, the Jensen. Jensen is the youngest of four children—he has three older sisters who doted on their baby brother—but Jenson's parents separated when he was seven, and his South African-born mother, Simone, mainly raised him.

With his father's support, he started karting at age eight and won practically every race he entered. At 11 years old and with an exceptional karting record, he won the British Cadet Kart Championship by scoring victories in all 34 races. He would eventually triumph twice more in the championship. He also won the Italian ICA Senior title in 1995, the European Supercup A Championship in 1997, (becoming the youngest driver ever to score the title) as well as the Ayrton Senna Memorial Cup. He switched from karts to cars in 1998, which brought about immediate success with Haywood Racing's Mygale as Button swept aside all contenders to take the British Championship crown. This awe-inspiring domination pushed him into the Formula Three arena by 1999, where he won two races and finished third and best-placed rookie in the British Championship, even though he was disadvantaged by racing with a Renault engine against the more-powerful Mugen-Hondas.

Exhibiting an extraordinary level of maturity and composure for such a young driver, Button

JENSON BUTTON 125

combined formidable speed with smoothness and aggression. Late in the '99 season, he was given his first taste of F1, courtesy of McLaren, as his prize for winning the prestigious McLaren Autosport BRDC Young Driver Award the previous season. That December he beat Jean Alesi's time in a 10-lap test run in Barcelona and was so impressive that team owner Sir Frank Williams decided it was time to give the youngster a tryout for the role of test driver. Jenson's astounding pace blew Brazilian teammate Bruno Junqueira out of the second race seat, and Button made a spectacular debut in Australia, matching or beating race times of teammate Ralf Schumacher. He scored a fourth-place finish at the German Grand Prix and then a fifth place in the Belgium, Austrian, Japanese and British Grands Prix and a sixth in the Brazilian Grand Prix, eventually finishing eighth in the 2000 Drivers' Championship, proving that he was worthy of the faith shown by his team owner.

As the new millennium dawned, Button became the shiny new "golden boy" of British racing and F1 had a new star. Few drivers have ever entered Formual One with the fanfare and media frenzy that surrounded the February 2000 announcement of Button as a Williams driver. He was splashed across the front pages of Britain's national daily newspapers and was stalked by paparazzi for Europe's celebrity gossip magazines.

However, on the business side of things, he was still overshadowed by Ralf Schumacher, and by the end of the year, Williams announced that Button would be replaced by Champ Car star Juan Pablo Montoya.

Jenson's father and his manager publicly vilified Montoya, opening calling him "stupid" and "hopeless" and even questioned Sir Frank's decision to "dump" Jenson. To many in the media as well as the fans, this behavior was extremely unprofessional. Jenson's star was now tarnished, and he was forced to look elsewhere for a ride.

Although still under contract to Williams, in early 2001 Button drove for Benetton, which had just been purchased by Renault, but he had a dismal season driving a car that was still under development and didn't perform as well as expected. The same could be said for Jenson. He did, however, manage a fifth place at the German Grand Prix but finished a disappointing seventeenth in the Drivers' Championship that year.

In 2002, new owner Renault renamed Benetton "Renault F1." Fortunately, team boss Flavio Briatore retained Button, but Italian teammate Giancarlo Fisichella was on the move and was replaced by Jordan's Jarno Trulli.

That season, Button had a much better performing car to drive, and he knew he had to make the most of this opportunity to impress. He needed to polish up that star again. He drove well, collecting 14 points to Trulli's nine and, though Trulli regularly outpaced him during qualifying runs, Button had, by far, the superior race pace. He narrowly missed taking third place and his first podium at the Malaysian Grand Prix when, because of suspension failure, Michael Schumacher passed him in the last lap; Button was forced to settle for fourth. The Brazilian Grand Prix gave him another fourth-place finish, and by year's end, he had secured seventh place in the Drivers' Championship.

The teammates were evenly matched, but by the end of the year, it was Button again who was shown the garage door. He was let go in favor of young Spanish star Fernando Alonso, whose star was rising almost as quickly as Button's had. But this time, Button's impressive racing style and new maturity was noticed by British American Racing (BAR) boss David Richards, who was looking for a replacement for Olivier Panis, and Button was signed in record time.

Flavio Briatore was the object of derision for making such a choice, but he was not the one eating crow when Alonso won the Drivers' Championship for Renault in 2005; Button remained winless and was again involved in another contract dispute.

Button joined the BAR team for the 2003 season, teaming up with former World Champion Jacques Villeneuve, but their relationship did not gel and they took the bad blood onto the track. Villeneuve ruined Button's points-finish in the first race of the year in Australia by pitting when it was Button's turn. This resulted in a "war of words" in the press between the two; however, as the season wore on, Button's times were consistently better than Villeneuve's. Unfortunately, Button crashed heavily during practice at Monaco, causing him to miss the race and the following testing session at Monza. The 180 mph smash took place during a morning practice session when his car crashed into a barrier, then spun sideways and hit a chicane. It was estimated that Button was pulling 30 Gs when he hit the second wall, which is enough force to distort facial features and cause internal organs to swell by 50 percent. But when the rescue crew cut him out of the wreckage, his first reaction was to laugh. As he stated afterwards, "I don't know why [I laughed], but that was my first reaction. It wasn't some kind of macho thing; perhaps it was relief or because the whole thing just seemed so ridiculous."

By the end of the season, Button's luck had once again turned around, and at the U.S. Grand Prix, he led a lap for the first time. He went on to finish ninth in the Drivers' Championship with 17 points; his teammate and track nemesis Villeneuve scored only six. By the end of the year, Villeneuve had moved on to another team and was replaced by Japanese driver Takuma Sato; Button was finally the number one driver.

In 2004, Button and BAR-Honda found themselves in heady company, almost at the top of the standings with only Michael Schumacher and Ferrari in front of them. Button scored a sixth place in the first race of the season, the Australian Grand Prix, after a sizzling qualifying session. Then in Malaysia, Button scored his first-ever podium finish with a third place. He found himself in the same position later at the inaugural Bahrain Grand Prix. In April, he secured his first pole position when he finished second at the San Marino Grand Prix, and by season's end, with 85 points to his name, he had allayed any doubts as to his potential for success as a serious contender for the F1 crown.

In mid-2004, it had been announced that Button would return to Williams in 2005, but BAR challenged the deal, and the Contract Recognition Board ruled in BAR's favor. So Button stayed put. The legal haggling and his supposed playboy lifestyle raised eyebrows in the sport. He purchased a luxury penthouse in Monaco, more as a tax shelter as many F1 drivers have, as well as maintaining his homes in Surrey, England, and Bahrain. He also bought a massive $2.5 million yacht christened "Little Missy" and found love in the guise of singer/actress and BBC reality TV show contestant Louise Griffiths, to whom he was engaged for two years before they separated in 2005.

Button had a poor start to the 2005 season, including a disqualification at the San Marino Grand Prix, after which he received a two-race ban. A dispute between Honda and Richards resulted in the veteran team leader being dismissed and replaced by an inexperienced Nick Fry. The much-anticipated challenge for the championship never materialized mainly because of unreliable engines and parts, and the team got caught up in the Michelin tire ban at Indy. This diminished the number of races BAR took part in, and Button only scored points in one race, the French GP.

That same year, Button again found himself in contractual deep water. Despite having signed an agreement to drive for the Williams team in the 2006 season, he judged the team's championship prospects were minimal because their engine suppliers, BMW, had purchased the Sauber team and were ceasing their supply of engines to Williams. Sir Frank Williams was unyielding and demanded the Button contract be honored despite Jenson's claim that circumstances had changed and he had a right to remain at BAR. Having bought out Button's contract from Williams for a reported $30 million, the BAR team confirmed September 21, 2005, that Button would drive for them in 2006 and would partner ex-Ferrari driver Rubens Barrichello.

The start of the 2006 season was a lot more promising with a fourth-place finish at the Bahrain

Grand Prix, securing him five points, and then a third place podium finish at the Malaysian Grand Prix. However, Jenson blew an engine on the last lap at the Australian Grand Prix, after setting a stunning pole position lap time. He was forced out of the race when he stalled just shy of the finish line.

In June 2006, to honor the Sportura Honda Racing F1 team, Seiko launched a new chronograph watch bearing the teams colors. Ever the fashion plate, Jenson introduced the stylish new wrist wear at a star-studded launch party and is featured in print ads for the timepiece. The watch bears the team emblem and is designed to withstand the rigors of team racing.

Off-track, Jenson Button has continued to raise media and fan awareness through guest appearances on TV, including a stint as an expert judge in a British TV show, *Be a Grand Prix Driver*. Many see this as misdirected ambition: perhaps he was more interested in fame and fortune that actually perfecting his on-track performances. However, at 26, he still has time to prove his critics wrong. He is more than capable of becoming Britain's latest "great hope" in Formula One, following in the footsteps of legendary drivers Mansell, Hill, Clark, Hunt, Surtees and Stewart. Not bad for a kid who failed his driver's test the first time out.

Chapter Seventeen

Kimi Räikkönen

BIRTH DATE: October 17, 1979

BIRTHPLACE: Espoo, Finland

RESIDES: Monaco

DRIVES: McLaren, Car #3

Some drivers just get no respect! How would you like a nickname that means "booger"? Many of Kimi Räikkönen's countrymen jokingly refer to the 27-year-old Formula One star as "Räkä," meaning "snot" in Finnish. Fortunately Kimi's other frequently used nicknames include less insulting ones, such as "Kimppa" or "Kimster," as he is called by his mechanics. Räikkönen is known as a calm, cool and calculating race strategist, which has prompted yet another nickname, "the Iceman."

Call him what you like—he is a major force in the world of Formula One and one of the most consistent championship contenders in recent years.

At the age of 10, Kimi Räikkönen started in national and international kart racing. After attaining considerable success in his teen years taking the titles in the Finnish Class A Championship, the Nordic Championship and the 1998 European Karting Grand Prix championship, he took up auto racing in 1999 at the age of 20.

For his first season, he competed in four races for Haywood Racing, finishing a respectable third in his first outing before being forced to withdraw from the next three because of technical problems. He was also lucky to secure a ride in the Formula Ford Euro Cup, where he finished fifth. Signing on with Manor Motor Sport, he won all of his first four starts, securing the Formula Renault Winter series.

Räikkönen stayed with Manor in 2000, competing in the British Renault Championship, where he took the title with relative ease after scoring seven wins out of 10 races and taking the podium after every race (seven pole positions and six fastest laps). Not bad for his sophomore season. During that same year, Kimi also competed in the Formula Renault series, where he notched up two wins, two poles and two fastest laps. For those keeping score, his stats reveal that out of the 23 races contested, Kimi had a success rate of more than 55 percent, winning a grand total of 13 races.

Based on his brilliant record, he got the nod from team owner Peter Sauber. Sauber gave Kimi his Formula One debut driving for the Swiss-based Sauber Petronas team in 2001, but not until the

FIA granted Kimi the necessary Super License; he had not gone through the normal evolution of first racing in F3 or F3000, so he needed to acquire special dispensation from F1's governing body.

His maiden season produced some outstanding performances that helped the team score their highest-ever finish, a fourth place in the Constructors' Championship. Despite the doubts surrounding his accelerated entrance into the sport, Kimi's strength behind the wheel and determination to win did not go unnoticed. He was wooed by McLaren to take the place of double world champion, Mika Hakkinen, who was planning to retire.

Throughout 2002, Räikkönen delivered some outstanding performances in his West McLaren Mercedes, out-qualifying his more experienced teammate David Coulthard on more than one occasion. The young Finn also came close to winning his first-ever race in Australia, but unfortunately he ran wide at one of the hairpin bends because of an oil spill on the track, allowing Michael Schumacher to cruise on by to victory.

Räikkönen's career exploded in 2003 when he posted 91 points to place second in the Drivers' Championship, missing out to Schumacher. He scored his first win in Malaysia, then secured seven second-place and two third-place finishes. But luck was not on Kimi's side going into the 2004 season.

The team started out with the new MP4-19 chassis, but before long, it was proven that the car simply was not competitive. As Kimi retired in one race after another with mechanical failures, it was clear to all that he was losing motivation. Mid-season, he was finally given a much more competitive 'b' specification chassis, which raised his game, and Kimi once more became a regular point scorer. Even with his dismal performance early on in the year, he managed to finish seventh in the overall standings, thanks to one victory coming his way at Spa-Francorchamps and a total of 45 points.

The 2005 season was a complete reversal of luck for the young, eager Finn, who came close to winning the championship. Kimi missed out on the title to Fernando Alonso without once making a significant error on the track. He was let down only because of the mechanical failures of his MP4-20 car. All told, he finished on the podium 12 times, including seven wins. Fans and proponents of Räikkönen argue that he was the best driver of the 2005 season, which was reflected in Räikkönen being given several post-season accolades from reputed magazines such as *F1 Racing* and *Autosport*, including the title Driver of the Season. The season also marked a couple of important

F1 records being set: Kimi shares the record of seven wins in a single season without winning the world title with four-time world champion Alain Prost, who initially set the record in 1984 and then matched it in 1988. Kimi also equaled Michael Schumacher's 2004 record of 10 fastest race laps in a single season.

Räikkönen's 2006 stats reflect another year of ups and downs, with a number of DNFs and continued technical problems with the McLaren cars. He ended the season in fifth place and Team McLaren Mercedes placed third in the Constructors' Championship. When Shumacher announced his retirement after completing the Italian GP, Ferrari named Räikkönen as his replacement. Räikkönen signed a three year contract with Ferrari and will partner with Felipe Massa.

Though never asleep at the wheel, Kimi does have a disconcerting habit of taking a snooze just prior to race time. In fact, at his maiden Grand Prix in Australia, teammates found him snoring away 20 minutes prior to the start command. He loves his catnaps so much that he needs to be woken up regularly before qualifying sessions and races.

Kimi resides in Switzerland with his wife, Jennie, and enjoys snowboarding, jogging, hockey and motorcross as well as regular workouts in his state-of-the-art gym.

Chapter Eighteen

Mark Webber

BIRTH DATE: August 27, 1976
BIRTHPLACE: Queanbeyan, New South Wales, Australia
RESIDES: Buckinghamshire, England
DRIVES: Williams-Cosworth, Car #9

This handsome 30-year-old "Thunder from Down Under" is the first Australian since David Brabham to race in Formula One. He made his grand prix debut in front of his home crowd in the Australian Grand Prix in 2002.

A native of Queanbeyan, New South Wales, Webber originally left Australia at the end of 1995 after competing in numerous karting events and the Australian Formula Ford championship. He made an impressive international debut with a third-place finish in the 1995 Formula Ford Festival at Brands Hatch in England. His performance prompted the famous Van Diemen Formula Ford team to sign him for the 1996 British Championship. Both Ayrton Senna and Eddie Irvine had driven for the team in their formative years, so Webber was following in some pretty famous footsteps. Webber finished runner-up in the series, and in 1997, he graduated to the British Formula Three Championship with a team headed up by fellow Australian Alan Docking.

Unfortunately Webber encountered sponsorship problems and was nearly forced to quit the series when the funding dried up. He managed to battle on when David Campese, the former Wallabies rugby union legend and an old mate from Webber's hometown, came to the rescue and personally financed Webber's next few races. Webber continued to deliver good results and was able to finish a respectable fourth in the series.

It wasn't long before his strong performances in the British series and various international F3 events attracted the attention of Mercedes boss, Norbert Haug, who invited Mark to test for the Mercedes AMG sportscar team.

The test was a resounding success, and Mark signed on with the team to compete in 1998's FIA GT Championship, partnering former F1 driver Bernd Schneider. Under Mercedes' guidance, Webber matured quickly and at the age of 20, working with a major manufacturer paid off big time.

The 1998 season was memorable for the Aussie. He undertook an extensive test program and a 10-round championship that took him to the U.S., Japan and Europe. He scored five wins, just missing

out on the title to teammates Klaus Ludwig and
Ricardo Zonta. In 1999, his career nearly came to
a premature end when he was involved in two
spectacular, high-speed crashes at the 24 Hours of
Le Mans race. An apparent aerodynamic fault with
the design of his Mercedes caused the cars of both
Webber and teammate Peter Dumbreck to somer-
sault, forcing Mercedes to withdraw its one
remaining car from the race and cease the remain-
der of the 1999 sports car campaign.

Although sidelined, Webber was determined to
get his career back on track for the following season, so he began working toward securing a ride
in the International Formula 3000 Championship
with Paul Stoddart's new European Formula Racing (EFR) team after he was introduced to Stoddart
by F1 team boss, Eddie Jordan.

In 2000, Fosters, the famed Australian brewer,
joined Yellow Pages as a personal sponsor for Mark
when he contested the International F3000 Championship. Mark blasted away the competition and
took the EFR team to victory in round two of the
series at Silverstone, taking an unexpected early
lead in the championship. He ended the season third
overall in the Drivers' Championship behind two
more-experienced drivers, Bruno Junqueira and
Nicolas Minassian, securing a place in the history
books as the highest-placed rookie that season.

His results earned him even more interest from industry insiders, this time from the Benetton PlayLife Formula One team, and in September 2000, Webber completed a successful three-day test for the team at Estoril in Portugal. This led to the team signing Webber on a long-term contract. For the 2001 season, Benetton contracted him to race for Super Nova Racing in Formula 3000 and to be the official test and reserve driver for the Benetton Renault F1 team.

Webber enjoyed another great season in 2001, with wins at Imola, Monaco and Magny Cours, and he finished runner-up in the F3000 series. Between races, he tested extensively for the Benetton Renault F1 team and contributed toward the team's end-of-season performance boost. Webber finally got the call to Formula One in 2002, when he joined the Minardi team to drive his maiden race in front of home fans in Melbourne. Mark drove the PS02 to fifth place, scoring two championship points, and the crowd went wild for the young Aussie.

Despite his brilliant opening run, Webber was unable to score any more points in 2002; however, he put in a dazzling performance at the Monaco GP, and this time Jaguar was watching. The Jaguar team bosses immediately snapped Webber up to partner with Antonio Pizzonia for the following season, and Webber enjoyed a good 2003 season, scoring 17 of the total 18 points amassed by the Jag team.

The 2004 race calendar lacked the luster of Mark's first season with Jaguar, who announced that the team was "for sale" mid-season. But Webber put in a workmanlike job for the team, qualifying second alongside Michael Schumacher at the Malaysian Grand Prix, where he unfortunately spun out of contention.

Yet another team boss was watching, and by the end of 2004, Sir Frank Williams signed Webber to join Nick Heidfeld in the BMW-powered Williams racing team in 2005. It was another tough season for the Aussie, who was a sensation in qualifying rounds but always seemed to fall short in the actual races, failing to score many points. Teammate Heidfeld was far more consistent, and Webber was left to pick up crumbs, scoring just one podium position at the Monaco GP and a 10th place in the overall standings for 2005.

Going into 2006, Webber remained with Williams and was joined by rising star and second-generation racer Nico Rosberg. Midway through the season, Webber hadn't delivered the sparkle he displayed in previous seasons, and though he expressed his desire to stay with the team through 2007, Williams announced on August 3, 2006, that they had decided to promote current test driver Alex Wurz to replace Webber. But the Aussie must have horseshoes up his exhaust, because within days, in fact 20 days prior to his 30th birthday, it was announced that Webber had been signed to the Red Bull Racing team for 2007, partnering the well-respected David Coulthard.

Always grateful for the chances he's been given, Webber welcomes the opportunity to give back to those who are not as fortunate as he is. He created the Mark Webber Pure Tasmania Challenge, a grueling six-day adventure race that combines cross-country trekking, mountain biking, road cycling and kayaking, to be held in Tasmania, Australia's rugged island state, in November 2006. The challenge is a major charity initiative to raise money for Victorian-based TLC For Kids and Cancer Council Tasmania's Cancer Plus program.

Mark enjoys every opportunity he gets to return home in between races. He resides full time with his girlfriend and his best four-legged friend, his dog Milo, in Buckinghamshire, England, but he doesn't mind the long flights back to Australia as long as it means he can enjoy a bit of R'n'R in the bush or some mountain biking, kayaking, trekking and the occasional game of tennis with his mates. He also enjoys a good game of Rugby Union, especially watching his beloved Wallabies national team.

He has eclectic musical tastes, listening to everything from Maroon 5 to Madonna to the Red Hot Chili Peppers, and he likes nothing better than to relax and read current affairs magazines or a good *National Geographic*.

With many years of driving still ahead, Webber aspires to build a career along the lines of Alain Prost or Michael Schumacher, tearing along his favorite tracks in Spa-Francorchamps, Monaco and Imola and especially in front of his loyal and noisy fans at home at the Australian Grand Prix.

Chapter Nineteen

Michael Schumacher

BIRTH DATE: January 3, 1969
BIRTHPLACE: Hürth-Hermülheim, Germany
RESIDES: Vufflens-le-Château, Switzerland
DRIVES: Ferrari, Car #5

Considered the greatest race driver of any Formula in the history of the sport, the 37-year-old Ferrari superstar has notched up an awesome list of records that surpass even the great Senna, widely regarded by many to be the fastest, most accomplished of the F1 racers until the 2006 season. Since Ayrton Senna's death in 1994, Schumacher has become the dominant driver of his era. However, the volatile German's driving tactics have had some critics and fans questioning his sportsmanship. It is common knowledge around the garage that Ferrari has issued standing team orders requiring Schumacher's teammates to concede to him on the track. But with this in mind, and regardless of the media and public's opinions concerning his worthiness, the driver's overwhelming successes have put Schumacher into the history books at the top of the list of all-time greats.

To put things in perspective, here are Schumacher's Formula One records:

Year	Record	#
2006	Most Race Wins	91
	Most Race Wins with One Team	72
	Most Podium Finishes	154
	Most Second Place Finishes	43
	Most Points Finishes	190
	Most Pole Positions	68
	Most Fastest Laps	76
	Most Race Wins from Pole Position	40
	Most Championship Points	1,369
2004	Most Championship Titles	7
	Most Consecutive Championship Titles	5
	Most Race Wins in a Season	13
	Most Consecutive Race Wins	7
	Most Fastest Las in a Season	10
	Most Championship points in a Season	148
	Most Triples (pole position, race win, and fastest lap)	20
2002	Most Podium Finishes in a Season	17

The "Red Baron," as Schumacher is often called, possesses a driving style that is often called into question, especially when considering his two most notable incidents: the 1994 Australian GP crash with Damon Hill and the European GP crash with Jacques Villeneuve in 1997.

One of Schumacher's most blatant disregards for a fellow competitor occurred at the 1994 Australian Grand Prix. Schumacher was barely leading Damon Hill; if Hill had won the race, he would have been that season's World Champion. As Hill applied pressure to Schumacher late in the race, the German made an error and ran wide off the track, crashing into a wall and damaging his car. Unbelievably Schumacher drove back onto the track, turning his ailing car straight into the side of Hill's vehicle as he passed. The impact damaged Hill's front suspension rods, forcing him out of the race and thus handing the title to Schumacher under highly controversial circumstances.

At the 1997 European GP, Schumacher was leading the race, followed closely by Jacques Villeneuve. The championship would be decided in circumstances similar to the 1994 incident: a win for either driver would guarantee him the World Championship. As the drivers approached a right-handed corner, Villeneuve tried to overtake Schumacher. As Villeneuve passed, Schumacher's car turned sharply into the side of his car. It is an accident that is still discussed and argued by both camps, but the FIA, Formula One's ruling body, judged it to be an act of dangerous driving. Schumacher's car was disqualified, and Villeneuve went on to finish third, behind Mika Häkkinen (his first F1 win) and David Coulthard, who were too far behind in the points to challenge Villeneuve for the championship. Schumacher was ultimately stripped of his second place in the final World Championship standings but retained his results and points for the season.

In recent years, Schumacher has made an effort to focus on winning races based solely on his driving skills, not bullying tactics; however, there are few races that go by without some protest or disagreement as to how he gets up on the podium yet again. But there is no disputing who is the king of Formula One—if the "Schu" fits...

Michael Schumacher, born in 1969 in Hürth-Hermülheim, Germany, began racing karts at the age of four, using a homemade kart built by his father, Rolf, who managed the local karting track. By age 12, Michael was granted his first license and began racing competitively. For the period from 1984 to 1987, Schumacher won numerous German and European kart championships, including the Formula Konig Series, in which he was so dominant that he had more or less cinched the title halfway through the season.

The following year, Schumacher moved on to the Formula Ford series, competing for two seasons in the German Formula Three series, grabbing the title in 1990 with five race wins then later topping that by also winning the international races at Macau and Fiji.

Throughout 1991, Schumacher continued his climb up the racing ladder, joining Mercedes' junior racing program in the World Endurance Championship. He won races in Mexico City and at Autopolis behind the wheel of a Sauber-Mercedes C291 and competed briefly in the Japanese Formula 3000 Championship, where he finished second, and the German Touring Car Championship. More importantly, 1991 was the year that Schumacher exploded onto the Formula One scene. He drove for Jordan-Ford in his maiden race in the Belgian Grand Prix as a replacement driver for Bertrand Gachot, who was jailed for spraying CS gas in a London taxi-driver's face. Team owner Eddie Jordan signed Schu after Michael assured him that he had lots of experience on the challenging Spa circuit. Fact was, he had only been around the track once—and that was riding on a borrowed bicycle! Though his expertise was strictly two-wheeled, Schumacher qualified his four-wheel ride in seventh place but unfortunately failed to complete the first lap because of clutch problems. That this was his only race for Jordan did not matter; Schumacher was quickly signed by the Benetton team.

After joining Benetton-Ford, he immediately showed great potential, becoming known as the up-and-coming driver to watch. In 1992, he finished third in the championship standings with eight podium finishes and 53 points. The following year was not quite so promising, but he did win one race. Williams once again dominated the 1993 field with only Senna able to challenge Alain Prost, who had the superior package in terms of engine, chassis and especially electronics. Nevertheless, 1993 was a critical year for developing the Benetton machine as electronic launch and traction controls were incorporated into their Engine Control Unit (ECU). It was also a critical year for developing Schumacher's career. He won in Portugal and placed fourth overall for the season. Then in 1994, Michael stunned the Grand Prix world when he left the legendary Senna in his dust, and after Senna's tragic death, Michael seemed unbeatable. But dark clouds swirled above him as Benetton was inundated with allegations of cheating. The team battled through all the disqualifications and bans, and eventually Michael beat Damon Hill to the title by one single point after the controversial accident at the last race in Australia. With nine more wins and a second championship crown, Schumacher moved over to the Ferrari team in 1996 and has stayed with them ever since.

That year, he brought home three wins for Ferrari and was more competitive the following year when he won in Monaco, France, Canada, Belgium and Japan, and then went into the final race in Jerez with a one-point advantage over Villeneuve. Again, controversy was Schu's co-pilot when he had his championship second place stripped from him by the FIA after his accident with Villeneuve.

The 1998 championship came down to the final race, but after he stalled from the pole position and blew a tire, Schumacher's chances of taking the title for a third time vanished into thin air. The 1999 season didn't get off to a good start either with problems in the opening race, but from then on, Michael quickly took the lead in the championship. Just when he thought he may finally take the title for Ferrari, he crashed at the British Grand Prix and suffered a severely broken leg that kept him out of racing for most of the season. He was able to return for the final two races and, though his teammate Eddie Irvine narrowly lost the Drivers' title, between them they were able to secure the first Constructors' Championship for Ferrari since 1983.

The new millennium dawned with Schumacher enjoying his best season ever. Ferrari partnered him with Rubens Barrichello, and after winning the first three races of the 2000 season, he captured his third world title and Ferrari's first Drivers' victory in 21 years at Suzuka, the second-last race of the season. The team also took the Constructors' crown.

Ferrari and Schumacher dominated 2001, with Michael tearing down numerous long-standing records and taking a fourth world title. He was now the record holder for Most Grand Prix Victories, surpassing Alain Prost's total of 52. With Fangio's record of five world titles well within his sights, Schumacher began the 2002 season with determination and an extremely strong, fast car. Fangio's record was finally equaled at the 11th race of the season, and as 2002 progressed, the German star kept rewriting the history books. The one dark blotch on the year came in Austria when team orders forced Barrichello to yield, handing Michael the win, which was greeted by loud booing fans as the world champion took to the podium.

Schumacher's sixth championship title came in 2003, followed by a seventh in 2004 when he blew away all competition by winning 12 of the first 13 races of the season as well as winning the final race in Japan.

Thanks to some FIA rule changes in 2005, Schumacher was finally toppled from his number one position in the sport. Bridgestone was struggling to produce a tire capable of lasting the entire race distance while at the same time maintaining grip like the product rival tire maker Michelin offered. This resulted in a frustrating season for both Ferrari and Schumacher, who only won a single race, the controversial U.S. Grand Prix where only the Bridgestone teams participated. Schumacher ended the season third in the championship standings, passing his title to the young Spanish driver, Fernando Alonso.

Many insiders anticipated Schumacher would retire after the 2006 season. After he won his fifth Italian Grand prix in early September 2006, Michael Schumacher confirmed the rumors that he would retire at the end of the season, and whatever the outcome of his championship battle with Alonzo, Schumacher ended his career holding just about all the records. He has seven World Championships under his belt, has driven 250 GPs and won 90, more than the combined wins of Senna, Clark and Fangio, and contributed to seven Constructors' titles. After Schumacher's emotional press conference, Team Ferrari announced that Kimi Räikkönen will replace Michael in 2007, a move that had been anticipated for several months leading up to the official announcements.

Apart from toppling all known F1 records, Schumacher has also won the coveted Laureus World Sportsman of the Year award twice, first in 2002 and again in 2004, for outstanding performances in the respective previous seasons. He joins a select group of sports stars to win this award, including golfer Tiger Woods, cyclist Lance Armstrong and tennis player Roger Federer. In the award's six-year history, no other sportsman has been nominated more times than Schumacher, who received five consecutive nominations (as well as the years he won, he was nominated in 2001, 2003 and 2005).

Married to Corinna Betsch in August 1995, Michael has two children, Gina-Maria and Mick. The family resides in Vufflens-le-Château, Switzerland, close to beautiful Lake Geneva, and Michael is protective of his private life, taking great efforts to keep his family away from the prying eyes of the media and over-zealous fans. His younger brother Ralf also drives in Formula One.

Now that he will no longer be busy on the track, Michael will have more time to pursue his many other sporting interests, including soccer, tennis, swimming and skiing. He also is dedicated to improving the lives of others and donated US$10 million to benefit victims of the 2004 tsunami. His bodyguard, Burkhard Cramer, and Cramer's two sons died while vacationing in Phuket, Thailand. Schumacher's generous donation surpassed that of any other sportsperson, most sports leagues, worldwide corporations and even some countries.

Following the 1997 race incident at Jerez, the FIA commandeered Schumacher to promote road safety as part of his disciplinary conditions. Although it was a short-term initiative, he is still an active advocate for road safety, and he participated in the global launch of FIA's Think Before You Drive campaign in 2005. He is also a special ambassador to UNESCO, personally donating US$3 million, funding projects for the construction of a school in Senegal, a clinic in Sarajevo and a center for street children in Peru. He visited Sarajevo to see how his support has benefited child victims of war, and for his contribution, he was named a UNESCO Champion for Sport in 2002.

There is no doubt that Schumacher is a wealthy man with an estimated annual salary in excess of US$80 million, including his endorsement deals. One such endorsement deal is with the German investment company Deutsche Vermögens-beratung, which is paying him US$8 million over a three-year period for simply wearing a four-inch logo on his post-race hat. Such is the power and glory of a World Champion F1 driver.

As he closed in on retirement, Schumacher began exploring other opportunities, and in early March 2006, it was reported that he would play a small role in the upcoming movie *Asterix at the Olympic Games*, alongside Real Madrid soccer stars David Beckham and Zinedine Zidane. Zidane, reluctant head-butting star of the year's World Cup, has just retired, and soccer's golden boy, Beckham, has also hinted of imminent retirement, stepping down as England's national team captain after the World Cup, so the film will feature a "holy trinity" of international sports stars and will doubtless become a cult classic in future years.

Chapter Twenty

Nico Rosberg

DATE OF BIRTH: June 27, 1985
BIRTHPLACE: Wiesbaden, Germany
RESIDES: Monte Carlo, Monaco
DRIVES: Williams-Cosworth, Car # 10

As Rosie O'Donnell would say, Nico Rosberg is a "real cutie-patootie"! The 21-year-old, blonde son of the Finnish 1982 Formula One champion, Keke Rosberg, was born June 27, 1985, in Wiesbaden, Germany and races under the German flag thanks to his mother's nationality. In fact, he speaks little Finnish while maintaining citizenship in both countries.

The elder Rosberg, known to race fans as "the Flying Finn," was and still is quite the firebrand who fought through the highs and lows of F1 to finally make the big time. In 1982 he became world champion with only one Grand Prix win to his name. By the time he retired from F1 he had competed in 114 Grands Prix, winning only five.

But those who remember Rosberg in action don't care about statistics—Keke was a phenomenon.

In the summer of 1985, Keke drove his turbo-charged Williams-Honda around Silverstone, breaking the average speed of 160 mph and creating a record that would stand for 17 years. But it meant little to Keke at that time; the greatest joy for him that summer was the birth of a little bundle of blond curls named Nico, his son and heir. And now, some 20 years later, that handsome kid is running the same tracks his dad did, racing for the Williams F1 team.

Nico seems very different from his father. He is quiet and shy when approached by the media and fans, not at all like dear old dad. But growing up in the shadow of such a famous father is not always easy, though Nico seems to be quite well adjusted and less troubled about it than some of his fellow second-generation F1 drivers.

At six years old, Nico had tried out karting at a public track and liked it. Keke bought his son his own kart by the time Nico was 10, but tennis was Nico's first foray into the international world of sports. When he was nine years old, Nico was playing tennis for the Monaco national team; in fact, he was pretty good at most ball games. Although his education was considered a priority (Nico had expressed a desire to study aerodynamics), he eventually decided to stick with racing rather than go to university.

In his early teens, Nico started racing in karts and quickly made a name for himself, chewing up the tracks and the competition. He advanced quickly to the German Formula BMW in 2002 and won the championship title confidently with nine victories in 20 races. He became the youngest man ever to drive a Formula One car when, at 17, he tested for Williams BMW. His superb performance resulted in a decision to drive for his father's team in the Formula Three Euroseries, which is a combination of several national Formula Three Championships that had existed prior to the EuroSeries formation. Nico's progress there was less impressive than he'd hoped, but he remained with the series until 2004. At the end of 2003, however, the Williams team took a much closer look at him than they had 12 months earlier. They decided to run Nico and Nelson Piquet Jr. in a test in Spain; however, the team eventually picked Antonio Pizzonia to be its test driver. The Williams team was still interested in the youngster, though, and they would come a-knocking again.

In 2005 Nico joined the ART Grand Prix team in the newly created GP2 Series. He enjoyed an excellent year that saw him capture the Drivers' Championship in the series. Then in November of the same year, the phone rang, and the Williams team reps were on the other end, this time with a much more positive response. Nico Rosberg was officially confirmed as a Williams F1 team driver for the 2006 season.

Even before the '06 season started, Nico was celebrating; he had set another record by attaining the highest-ever score in Williams' Engineering Aptitude test. In his first Formula One race in Bahrain, he not only placed in the points (he placed seventh behind teammate Mark Webber), he also recorded the fastest lap, an amazing achievement considering that he was driving a car that was not thought to be competitive enough to get him to the podium. He'd also had to fight his way through the field after losing the car's nose-cone on the first lap of the race. The rookie then qualified third at the 2006 Malaysian Grand Prix, but during the race his Cosworth engine blew up after only seven laps.

Because he is so media-shy, there aren't many inside stories about Nico's personal life. He plays his cards close to the vest and little is known of his home life. He has, however, recently acquired a beautiful girlfriend, Viviane, a 21-year-old German student who keeps a low profile at the race tracks while Nico, very much a female fan favorite, receives more than his fair share of whistles and cheers as he walks along pit row. His boyish charm and Brad Pitt-like good looks make him a natural for magazine pin-up shots and numerous websites. There is no denying his Scandinavian roots; however, he finds himself in a rather unusual situation as a non-Finnish-speaking Finn. He was born in Germany and enjoyed a privileged upbringing in Monaco and Ibiza.

Nico was too young to remember his father when Keke was at the peak of his F1 career. In fact, Keke retired at the end of 1986, when Nico was 18 months old, but during the mid-1990s, Keke raced in DMT (Audi/German Touring Car racing) and Nico often went to races. Now the roles are slightly reversed. Throughout his fledgling career, Nico has been managed by his father, though there is no formal contract between them. The one-time champion Keke has been careful to stay in the background, allowing his son to enjoy the limelight. With two successful podium finishes already under his belt in the first half of his rookie season, Nico Rosberg should have more than his fair share of that limelight in the coming seasons.

Chapter Twenty One

Rubens Barrichello

BIRTH DATE: May 23, 1972

BIRTHPLACE: São Paulo, Brazil

RESIDES: São Paulo, Brazil

DRIVES: Honda Racing, Car #11

Brazilian-born Rubens Barrichello had one of the most rapid climbs from karting to Formula One of any active driver. He had won five national karting titles by the time he was 17, and in 1990, he went to Europe to race the Formula Lotus series. In his first year, he won the championship, a feat he replicated the following year in the British Formula Three Championship, beating young British driver, David Coulthard. Barrichello very nearly joined Formula One when he was 19 but instead chose to join Formula 3000, winning the title in 1991 for West Surrey Racing. By his 21st birthday, however, he was ready to make the move to Formula One.

Barrichello made his F1 debut in 1993, driving for the Jordan team at the South African Grand

Prix, where he qualified 14th. Were it not for fuel problems late in the race, he would have finished his third race in second place behind his hero and countryman, Ayrton Senna. Although Barrichello improved throughout the season, his career nearly ended in tragedy at the San Marino Grand Prix, where a violent crash during practice knocked him unconscious, nearly killing him. On the track, Dr. Sid Watkins' quick thinking saved Rubens' life, preventing the racer from swallowing his own tongue. Rubens' spirits were damped even further when his mentor, Ayrton Senna, died at the race two days later. Barrichello never truly recovered that season. He did manage to earn a pole position at the rain-soaked Spa-Francorchamps—the youngest driver at the time to earn one—but unfortunately spun out in lap 19. He finished a respectable sixth in the Drivers' Championship, and that same year he notched up a third-place finish at the Pacific GP and scored five more fourth places.

The 1995 season saw Barrichello suffer numerous mechanical failures, but at the Canadian GP, he notched up his first second-place finish. He remained with the Jordan team until the 1997 season when, after his relationship with team owner Eddie Jordan soured, he left for the newly formed Stewart Grand Prix team. Although finishing second at Monaco in Stewart's inaugural year, Barrichello struggled in his first two years with Jackie Stewart's team, but after an impressive season end, he managed to finish seventh in the 1999 Championship. This was enough for Scuderia Ferrari to sign Barrichello as their number two driver behind Michael Schumacher for the 2000 season, replacing Eddie Irvine. So confident was Barrichello that he actually referred to himself as the team's "1b" driver.

The 2000 season was groundbreaking for Rubens, and it was a year he will never forget. In Hockenheim, Germany, he achieved his first victory, despite having started way back in the grid in 18th position; it was his 128th race, the longest wait for a driver's first win. This first career victory brought tears to his and many of his fans' eyes as he stood on the top step of the podium for the first time. His heroic efforts throughout the season helped Ferrari clinch the title in the Constructors' Championship, while the Brazilian finished fourth overall in the Drivers' battle.

Although no further victories were forthcoming in the 2001 season, Rubens battled it out for second place in the Drivers' Championship with old friend and McLaren driver David Coulthard, but he failed to beat out the Scot and had to settle for third.

His success continued throughout 2002 thanks to Ferrari's dominance of Formula One: he managed to finish second behind Schumacher in the 2002 championship, as Ferrari expanded its lead over the rest of the field. Four resounding wins came his way, the most notorious being the win at the U.S. Grand Prix when, together with teammate Michael Schumacher, the pair attempted to create history by crossing the line with the tiniest gap between cars in F1 history. Unfortunately, it didn't work out as planned, and Rubens took the victory away from Schumacher by a narrow margin. Team orders allowed Barrichello to earn the four victories, with Schumacher trailing him each time by less than a second. Similar team orders also forced the Brazilian to yield several potential victories to Schumacher, including the 2002 Austrian Grand Prix, where he pulled over at the last turn of the race. This blatant manipulative behavior eventually led to team orders being banned by officials in 2003.

Rubens suffered a relatively poor 2003 season by Ferrari standards as both Kimi Räikkönen and Juan Pablo Montoya forced the Brazilian into fourth place, while teammate Michael Schumacher notched up another championship title.

Barrichello finished second behind Schumacher in seven of the first 13 races of 2004, but won both the Italian and the Chinese Grands Prix, clinching a championship second place. He finished the year with an impressive 114 points and an unbelievable 14 podiums finishes, just one behind Schumacher.

But both the Ferrari teams struggled throughout 2005. The Bridgestone-Ferrari package was a dud, and Rubens would climb the podium only four times on his way to a disappointing eighth position in the championship. But the Bridgestone vs. Michelin tire issue was just a minor concern compared to the situation with teammate Schumacher. Rubens was becoming increasingly troubled by team instructions to allow Schumacher to take the lead, so in August of that year, he announced he would depart Ferrari at the end of 2005 to join Honda F1.

As he started the 2006 in a new ride, Rubens struggled to master his car and was repeatedly outpaced by his new teammate, Jenson Button. Barrichello claimed the car did not suit his driving style, and after modifications to the car were completed, he was back on track and competitive. At the 2006 Monaco Grand Prix, he nearly got his first podium for the Honda team, but after he accidentally sped through pit lane, he was given a drive-through penalty that destroyed his hopes for a maiden team win.

The one win he's always longed for still seems beyond his grasp—a win at home for his loyal Brazilian fans. Barrichello has been unlucky on his home turf, failing to finish 10 of the 13 Brazilian GPs in which he has competed; his best result was a third place in 2004. Now, being out from under the shadow of Schumacher, "Rubinho," as he is known to his countrymen, finally has his chance to shine.

Rubens is as dedicated to his family as he is to racing. He and his wife, Silvana, have two sons, five-year-old Eduardo and Fernando, born in 2005.

Chapter Twenty-Two

Scott Speed

BIRTH DATE: January 24, 1983
BIRTHPLACE: Manteca, California
RESIDES: Fuschl am See, Austria
DRIVES: Torro Rosso, Car # 21

In 2006, 23-year-old San Jose, California-born Scott Speed completed a meteoric rise, overcoming a career-threatening disease as well as the culture shock of relocating to Europe to become the first American to race in Formula One since Michael Andretti got behind a wheel in 1993.

Raised in Manteca, California, Speed began mapping out a career in Formula One at age four after attending a weekend kart race at Sears Point Raceway with his father, Mike. The youngster went home and immediately sketched a detailed layout of the 11-turn road course with his crayons. The map was so precise that his parents were sure he had copied it from a magazine with an aerial view. After searching the house high and low for the non-existent publication, they realized young Scott had drawn the track from memory, including the elevation changes and even the location of the restrooms. His mother, Julie, has often joked about the incident, saying that although he wasn't even in kindergarten at the time, Scott's innate sense of direction has since allowed him to map out a career in racing that few have traveled.

As with most auto-racing careers, Scott started off in karts, driving in his first event when he was nine. Within two years, he had scored his first national championship title and then went on to win numerous titles and championships between 1996 and 2001. He became the only karter to ever win two Super Nationals, which he achieved consecutively in 2000 and 2001. Scott then made his single-seater debut in 2001, contesting the Jim Russell Racing Championship and winning the series in his first attempt.

The following season, he experienced great success in the Skip Barber National Championship and also contested several rounds of the Formula Mazda Championship, which brought him to the attention of the Red Bull Driver Search, an initiative launched to discover America's young racing talent. As quickly as his name implies, Scott Speed was in the run-offs against some of the country's outstanding young drivers and eventually succeeded in winning the inaugural program.

One benefit for winning the Red Bull Driver
Search was a season in the prestigious British F3
Championship, driving for the Alan Docking
Racing team as well as the Formula Renault
German championship. He excelled in the European ladder series, winning Formula Renault
Championships and finishing third in GP2. But
fate dealt Scott a cruel hand when he was stricken
with ulcerative colitis, a debilitating intestinal
inflammation that causes bleeding and loss of
bowel control. Unfortunately, this meant that he
had to sit out a number of races. After 18 months,
Speed almost had his colon removed before a new
treatment was applied that finally sent the disease
into remission.

Scott was able to resume racing in 2004, contesting the Formula Renault championships in both
Germany and Europe with the German-based
Motopark Academy. In addition to winning both
championships, thus becoming the first-ever
American to win a European Junior Formula
Championship, he also tested for Red Bull's Eddie
Cheever's IRL IndyCar team, contributing important feedback for the team. He went on to join the
new GP2 series in 2005 with iSport International,
and though he never won any rounds of the championship, Scott was a regular visitor to the podium,
finishing that season in third position behind Nico
Rosberg and Heikki Kovalainen. Scott also got his
first taste of F1 in late March 2005, when he tested

the Red Bull car at Barcelona. He topped the timesheets, outpacing established Williams F1 drivers Nick Heidfeld and Antonio Pizzonia, as well as fellow Red Bull tester, Neel Jani.

Then in early June, following another brief but successful test, it was announced that Scott would get behind the wheel of the third car in the Friday free-practice sessions at both the Canadian and United States Grands Prix. Over the subsequent winter months, Scott gained further experience and mileage by participating in a number of rounds of another inaugural series, the A1 Grand Prix World Cup of Motorsport. He logged a personal best result of fourth in the feature race at Estoril.

With the perfect American racing hero name, Scott Speed is poised to become the Formula One "savior" of the United States. Team sponsor Red Bull is obsessed with penetrating the gigantic U.S. market and getting into Formula One (they are already running teams in NASCAR); their goal is to deliver the first U.S. World Champion since Mario Andretti in 1978. But Speed will face a steep learning curve in 2006. As the new Red Bull Squadra Toro Rosso outfit, Speed and his teammate Tonio Liuzzi are the only team running restricted V10 engines. Until FIA is able to create a fair balance between the V10s and V8s, it will be difficult to compare Scott's track performances to his rivals, and it certainly will be interesting to see how he measures up to the hot-shot Italian Liuzzi.

But for all the glowing kudos and future prospects, Speed has many detractors, especially in the media and on the track. His recent temper tantrums and post-race outbursts, especially after a disastrous Melbourne GP, have resulted in fines, the loss of his first F1 championship point by race officials and numerous news stories that focus more on his volatile personality than on his driving abilities.

In a recent newspaper article, Speed was quoted as stating that he agrees, "...fundamentally, I'm self-centered, I'm arrogant and very competitive, and those three things make it quite difficult to deal with me off the track. But they're definitely the reasons I've gone so far in racing."

He is undoubtedly the best U.S. road racer of his generation and has repeatedly impressed everyone on the GP2 circuit, taking one pole, five podiums and five fastest laps. Sir Jackie Stewart, a three-time F1 champion, believes success by Speed would mean "new life for F1 in America." Says Speed, "I want to do what I can to bring F1 to America as much as I can. I love it so much I want to share it with my country."

Since the 2005 U.S. Grand Prix debacle where fans booed and left the track in droves following the conflict with the tire suppliers, which resulted in nearly all of the teams withdrawing from the race,

Formula One had lost its glitter and appeal. But during Speed's recent U.S. debut at Indianapolis Motor Speedway, there were glimpses of the impact he could have on restoring the F1 fan base in his native country. On the first day of practice, seven American flags and banners reading "USA 4 Speed" and "In Scott We Trust" waved in the grandstands facing his team's garage bay.

Like most other F1 drivers, though, Speed lives in Europe, conveniently close to the prestigious 18-race international circuit, which stops in 16 countries from Bahrain to Malaysia to China, and to a worldwide fan base estimated in the hundreds of millions.

He owns a lake house in the Austrian town of Fuschl am See near Salzburg, where he trains at a facility owned by team sponsor Red Bull. Since moving overseas, he has also acquired a slight accent and jokes that he speaks "Valentinenglish" as a result of having a beautiful Austrian girlfriend named Valentina, who speaks four languages.

But in any language, and regardless of his long-overdue improved track etiquette, Scott Speed has more than proven himself worthy and is poised for an exciting 2006 season.

Chapter Twenty-Three

Takuma Sato

DATE OF BIRTH: January 28, 1977
BIRTHPLACE: Tokyo, Japan
RESIDES: Daytona Beach, Florida and Monaco
DRIVES: Super Aguri F1, Car #22

Twenty-nine-year-old, Tokyo-born Takuma Sato always dreamed of becoming a speed demon on the world's most prestigious auto racing circuits. His homeland, however, offered few opportunities for the fledgling racer, whose first experience with anything speedy was racing bicycles as a teenager.

Saving all his minor competition winnings, Sato scraped together enough money in 1996 to purchase a kart, and in 1997, entered a scholarship competition to enter the Honda Suzuka Racing School. Sato won his scholarship and developed his skills under the guidance of the esteemed manufacturer. The scholarship also included a fully paid drive in the 1998 All-Japan Formula Three Championship, but Sato decided to pass on this opportunity to pursue his desire of driving Formula One. However, to achieve this prize, he would have to pack his bags and go to Europe.

He headed west in mid-1998, finding a home with the small but respected Diamond Racing team. He contested a handful of Formula Vauxhall Junior races, then at the end of the year graduated with Diamond to Formula Opel. Sato started his first full year of car racing in 1999, taking sixth place in the hotly contested EFDA Formula Opel Euroseries. He also competed in the last few rounds of the British F3 Championship in Class B, where he won the Macau Grand Prix support race for AF2000 cars with the Meritus Team.

Sato signed on with Carlin Motorsport for 2000 to compete in the F3 'A' class, easily winning five races and taking third place in the British Championship. By now, he had been noticed by Grand Prix teams, and in December, Sato got his first taste of the big time when he was asked to test in F1 with both Jordan GP and British American Racing. BAR signed him as their test driver for 2001, and he also became contracted to Honda for the first time.

Sato remained in F3 throughout 2001, starting the season as clear favorite for the British championship. He dominated the championship and broke the record for the number of wins in the British F3 Championship with 12 out of 13 possible victories. He then secured first place in the

Marlboro Masters of F3 at Zandvoort and the International race supporting the British Grand Prix. He also impressed the BAR team with his test outings at Silverstone and Mugello.

Takuma, or "Taku" as he's called by family and fans, ended his stint in F3 with a bang when he won the Macau Grand Prix in November 2001. With victories in both the preliminary qualifying event and the main race, he sent a clear message that he was ready for the big leagues. His outstanding talent earned him a seat in Formula One when he signed a deal with the Jordan Grand Prix team in 2002.

It was a dramatic first year for Sato. He was partnered with the highly rated Italian Giancarlo Fisichella, but it was a season of highs and lows that ended with Takuma Sato scoring his first F1 points in a sensational race at Suzuka, where he came home in fifth place. Throughout the season, Taku proved to be fast but erratic and prone to crashes. He hit an early career low point when he was involved in a horrendous crash in Austria that destroyed both his car and that of Nick Heidfeld, who actually caused the crash. Sato suffered a minor concussion and was unable to leave the car for several minutes because his legs were trapped.

In 2003, as the BAR team's third driver, Sato played a key role in the development of the Honda-powered BAR Honda 005 and 006 race cars. And just like in a Hollywood movie script, Sato rode in on his shining charger to save the day when, for the final race of the year, at the last minute he substituted for regular race driver Jacques Ville-neuve at Suzuka, scoring two points with a fantastic drive to fifth place.

Sato secured the full-time race seat for 2004 with the BAR team and entered his second full year of F1 racing with a much improved team and car. Early testing suggested that the BAR Honda 006 would be a strong performer—and so it was. Sato proved very fast from the outset, but his season declined as his car was beset by of a series of mechanical and engine problems. His teammate Jenson Button scored great podium finishes but Sato was not so fortunate. For Sato, eighth position in the championship was a reasonable result, his best race finish coming with a third place at the U.S. Grand Prix at Indianapolis. Sato also achieved a commendable second place in qualifying for the European Grand Prix, behind only Michael Schumacher. This helped give BAR a second-place finish in the Constructors' Championship.

Heading into the 2005 season, the pressure was on Sato to raise his game still further and take the challenge to teammate Button. But Sato had a disastrous season. His car had a 007 chassis mated with the Honda power plant, resulting in a non-competitive car. Sato's season ended with an embarrassing single championship point to his name. His entire team was disqualified from the San Marino GP and banned for two more races for allegedly cheating. The final races of 2005 saw pressure mounting for Sato, and after several mistakes on track at his home event in Japan and then again at the Chinese GP, BAR Honda dropped the Japanese driver in favor of Rubens Barrichello for the 2006 season.

Sato's F1 career appeared doomed. But once more his dream was kept alive when the fledgling Super Aguri F1 team called on him for a fresh start to the new season. Super Aguri is a small but enthusiastic new team, and Sato now has a chance to show his undeniable talent and true potential. After the early races of the 2006 season, Sato has comfortably outpaced rookie teammate Yuji Ide, and his erratic driving habits have diminished. Sato seems to have found his niche, and the heartthrob of Japanese racing is maturing into a well-rounded sportsman. To add to Sato's motivation for the new season, in late 2005, his wife gave birth to their son in Monaco, where they reside much of the year.

A popular personality during fan meet-and-greets, Sato has enjoyed an ever-growing celebrity status at home. Fans chant his name, wear his merchandise and collect souvenirs by the millions of yen. The 2006 movie *Fast & Furious:Tokyo Drift*, though not involving Formula One, has illuminated the enthusiasm for auto sports in Japan, and thousands of young men (and women) dream of a career behind the wheel. Takuma Sato makes an ideal role model for them to honor.

Chapter Twenty-Four

Tiago Monteiro

DATE OF BIRTH: July 24, 1976

BIRTHPLACE: Porto, Portugal

RESIDES: Porto, Portugal

DRIVES: Midland (MF1), Car #18

Portuguese driver Tiago Monteiro is not your everyday, garden-variety F1 racer; his is a career that is unique, rich and varied. Unlike most auto racers, he did not start his career on kart tracks as a young boy, nor did he have his parents re-mortgage their house to fund his passion. In fact, he didn't get behind the wheel of a race car until the age of 20, and that was just for fun. Tiago turned that "fun" into an exciting career, starting with a win at the Porsche Carrera Cup Championship. He was then crowned Rookie of the Year in 1997. Monteiro had caught the racing bug, and he has never since looked back.

In fact, by the 2005 United States Grand Prix, Tiago had achieved the goal of becoming the most successful Portuguese driver ever in Formula One racing history. And by the time of the 2005 Belgian Grand Prix, Tiago had finished every race of the 2005 season, taking the record for consecutive finishes for a rookie driver in F1, wresting that title away from the legendary Jackie Stewart, who finished his first eight races.

The Monteiro family had been involved in the hotel management business for many years, and young Tiago was set to follow in his father's footsteps. He had just acquired a diploma in hotel management, but after his initial taste of speed, his destiny took a sharp turn toward a career in racing. Tiago had paid a visit to the Paul Ricard circuit in France with his father in 1996, where the elder Monteiro was to test a Porsche. Watching his father whiz around the track, Tiago found it impossible not to indulge in a lap around the circuit himself. Accompanied by a chaperon— professional driver Luc Rozentvaig—he impressed everyone present with his innate skills and instincts, especially because he was driving on wet asphalt after a heavy rainfall. As a result of his track expertise, his father enrolled him in an upcoming competition, and Tiago took part in his first race the following year, the French Porsche Carrera Cup championship.

It didn't take long for the young rookie from Porto—the major city north of Lisbon and home to the country's port wine industry—to experience the sweet taste of success. He learnt everything about the category, the car and the circuits, and soon Tiago began to garner praise, winning the Group B Championship on his first attempt. He also nailed five wins as well as becoming the series Rookie of the Year. Despite his late start, Tiago sped through the ranks and the following year, conquered the lofty French Formula Three Championship for Team Signature Compétition. This was his first entry into a single-seater championship, and he landed at the foot of the podium twice, again winning the honor of being named Rookie of the Year.

In 1999, the Portuguese driver changed teams, completing his education in F3 with the Adam Sharpe Motorsport(ASM) team, one of the top teams in French F3, the current Euroseries and GP2. Continuing in the championship in 1999, Tiago captured one win and three other podiums to finish fifth overall. As well as the F3 program, Monteiro drove in GT championship tests, hoping to expand his range of technical knowledge and get the maximum amount of experience possible. He also competed in the 24 hours of Le Mans, finishing 16th overall and sixth in the GT2 class. In the International Renault Finals held at the Portuguese circuit in Estoril, Monteiro claimed the win after taking pole position and the fastest lap of the race.

In 2000, Monteiro again competed in French F3, winning four times throughout the season and finishing second in the championship. He also competed in the single Formula Three European Championship double-header race and ended up in second place overall with one win at Circuit de Spa-Francorchamps. Racing in a couple of all-star events, he scored a second place in the Korea Super Prix and a ninth at the famous Macau Grand Prix. At the Lamborghini Super Trophy series, he managed to turn in the fastest lap at Magny-Cours, and both the pole position and the fastest lap at Laguna Seca.

Moving ahead to 2002, Monteiro was busy developing a great on-track reputation with a second-place finish in the French F3 Championship after taking six poles, four wins and four podiums. Always the multi-tasker, he competed in the French GT Championship where he landed four pole positions, two class wins and five podium finishes in the GTB class. He won both races in the Formula France series, and in the Andros Trophy race, he drove the fastest lap with a best finishing position of fourth. He had moved up to the Formula 3000 International Championship with the Super Nova Racing team, taking five top-ten finishing positions on his way to 12th place in the championship standings. Tiago got his first taste of Formula One in 2002 as he completed the Renault

F1 Driver Development Scheme, testing with the Renault team at Barcelona.

In 2003, he signed on with Fittipaldi Dingman Racing for the Champ Car World Series and achieved a pole position in Mexico City. He then lead two races, finishing out the season with 10 top-10 finishes and scoring 29 points to give him a 15th-place finish in the championship.

In 2004, Monteiro signed up as an official Minardi test driver for the season. He also competed in the Nissan World Series with Carlin Motorsport and was named Rookie of the Year after finishing second in the championship. As the cherry on top of all the racing whipped cream, he was ranked fifth in *Autosport* magazine's Top 10 Drivers in the Formula One "breeding ground" championships.

But 2005 marked Monteiro's big break into Formula One as a race driver with the Jordan Toyota team. Teaming up with the highly rated Indian driver, Narain Karthikeyan, Monteiro had a solid first season, taking the spotlight away from his teammate. Monteiro was the model of consistency and made it to the checkered flag in all but one Grands Prix. At the Brazilian Grand Prix, however, engine failure brought his run of success to end. Despite this, he still managed to break the record for the most finishes in a single season. The volatile Michael Schumacher finished all 17 races of the 2002 season, while both Monteiro and Rubens Barrichello finished 17 out of 18 races in 2004. Tiago's 11th place at the 2005 Chinese Grand Prix meant that he had finished 18 out 19 races.

The 2005 U.S. Grand Prix, however, was a farcical affair. Only the six teams using the Bridgestone tires competed when, because of safety concerns, all of the Michelin-equipped teams pulled out of the race, not taking their place on the grid. But Monteiro seized his chance and followed home the Ferrari duo of Michael Schumacher and Rubens Barrichello to claim the third place podium position in what was just his ninth F1 start. He went on to score another point with a fine drive to eighth position at Spa-Francorchamps to close out a superb year of F1 racing.

For the 2006 season, Midland resigned Monteiro to partner Christijan Albers, and at time of writing, they are placed 20th and 22nd respectively in the points standings. Both need some podiums in the remaining races of the season to put them in back into future championship contention.

Notoriously private with his personal life, Tiago has a lovely blue-eyed, brunette girlfriend, who often accompanies him trackside; however, little is known of any plans for nuptials.

Glossary of F1 Terms

Armco barrier

The metal barrier fitted at the sides of race tracks designed to absorb a high speed impact and prevent the car from crashing into spectators or, in the case of the Monaco Grand Prix circuit, into the harbor

Aerofoil or wing

Attached at the rear of the car, used to keep the car firmly on the track at high speed by providing maximum downforce

Ballast

Weights fixed on cars to maximize balance and bring them up to the minimum weight requirement

Bargeboard

A piece of bodywork mounted vertically between the front wheels and the side pods to help even out the airflow around the sides of the car, making it more aerodynamic

Black flag

A black flag accompanied by a car number directs a driver to return to his pit and is most often used to signal to the driver that he has been disqualified from the race

Black with orange circle flag

This flag accompanied by a car number warns a driver that he has a mechanical problem and must return to his pit.

Blue flag

A blue flag warns the driver that he is about to be lapped and to let the faster car overtake him. If a driver passes three blue flags without complying, then the driver risks being penalized. Blue lights are also displayed at the end of the pit lane when the pit exit is open, and a car on track is approaching.

Bottoming

When a car's chassis hits the track surface sometimes making sparks fly. This happens because the suspension has hit the maximum amount of compression it can take, usually because of increased downforce.

Chicane

A tight sequence of corners in alternate directions, such as in an S-shape. It is usually inserted into a circuit to slow down the cars, often just before a high-speed corner or straightaway.

Diffuser

The rear section of the car's floor or undertray, through which the air flowing under the car exits. The design of the diffuser is important, because it controls the speed at which the air exits and thus changes the aerodynamics of the car. The faster the exit, the lower the air pressure beneath the car and the more downforce the car generates, creating more grip.

DNF

Did Not Finish—a car does not complete a race

Downforce

The aerodynamic force that forces a car downwards, improving the car's traction and handling through corners. Depending on the circuit layout, it can have high or low downforce, forcing drivers to adjust accordingly with different tires or driving styles.

Drive-through-penalty

One of two penalties that can be handed out at the discretion of the Stewards during the race. With this penalty, drivers must enter pit lane, drive through it complying with the speed limit and rejoin the race without stopping.

Drag

The air resistance a car experiences as is goes forward

FIA

Stands for the *Fédération International d'Automobile*, the ruling body of worldwide motorsport, based in Switzerland

Flat Spot

An area of a tire that is worn heavily only in one spot, occurring frequently after extreme braking or during a spin. A flat spot in the tire impedes the car's handling, often causing severe vibration and in many cases forces the driver to pit for new tires.

Formation lap

The single lap around the circuit just before the start of the race. After the lap, cars are stopped again on the grid in their starting formation, ready for the command to start. Sometimes drivers use this lap to warm up their tires, which explains why they drive their vehicles in a wavy pattern.

Gravel trap

A patch or lane of gravel on the outside of corners designed to stop cars that misjudge a corner or spin off. Sometimes drivers are able to rejoin the race after spinning into the gravel trap.

Green flag

A green flag gives the all clear. When a driver has passed a danger point on the track and prohibitions imposed by yellow flags have been lifted, he can then safely resume racing.

Half black, half white flag

This flag, accompanied by a car number, warns of unsportsmanlike conduct; it may be followed by a black flag if the driver does not observe the warning

Installation lap

A lap done upon arrival at a circuit, where drivers can test their car functions, such as throttle, brakes and steering, before heading back to the pits without crossing the finish line

Jump start

A driver moves off his grid position before the five red lights have been switched off to signal the start of the race. Sensors on the circuit detect premature movement of any car, and a penalty is imposed on the driver.

Monocoque

The one-piece "tub" where the driver's cockpit is located. The engine is located behind it and the front suspension on either side at the front.

Nomex

The fire-resistant material used to make the driver's suits, gloves and shoes

Paddles

F1 cars do not have gear sticks like commercial cars, and drivers use small flat levers (or paddles) on either side of the steering wheel to change gears. One paddle is for changing gears up and the other is for downshifting.

Parc Ferme

Literally meaning "close park," this is a fenced-off area into which cars are driven after qualifying and then completing the race. In this area, no team members are allowed to touch the cars except under the strict supervision of race stewards (the F1 equivalent of NASCAR's "impound" rule).

Pole position

The first place on the starting grid, which is awarded to the driver with the fastest lap time during the qualifying session

Qualifying or qualifying session/race

The one-hour sessions one or two days prior to the race in which drivers are allowed to drive laps to set the best time they can. The fastest driver of the qualifying session prior to the race takes pole position.

Racing line

An imaginary line around a circuit that has been proven to be the most efficient and quickest route around the circuit

Red flag

A red flag indicates that the race has been stopped due in most cases to an accident or poor track conditions (poor weather, especially rain or fog)

Scrutineering

The technical checking of race cars by the officials before and after the race to make sure the cars comply with all the regulations and specifications

Sidepods

The part of the car that makes up the mono-coque's sides, installed alongside the driver's seat and running back to the rear wing. It also houses the radiators.

Slipstreaming

An aerodynamics term where a driver is able to catch the car ahead of him and use the air coming off the car in front to reduce drag on his car, allowing the driver to achieve a higher speed and sling-shot past the car in front (same as "drafting" in NASCAR)

Splash and dash

A very quick pit stop normally during the final laps of a race when a driver makes a pit stop just to add a few gallons of fuel to his car to make sure he can finish the race

Steward

One of three high-ranking officials at each race appointed to make decisions to ensure drivers and teams adhere to FIA regulations. Stewards have the discretion to hand out penalties to drivers and teams during and after the race.

Stop-and-go-penalty

One of two penalties that can be handed out to a driver at the discretion of the Stewards during the race. This penalty forces the driver to make a pit stop, remain stationary for 10 seconds, but he is not allowed to take on fuel or change tires during this period. After 10 seconds he is allowed to resume the race.

Tear-off strips

Each driver has several layers of see-through plastic film covering the visor of their helmets that they can tear off as the visor gets dirty during the race

Traction

The degree to which a car is able to transfer its power onto the track surface, which can vary depending on track surface, weather or tire conditions

Traction control

A means of electronically reducing the power to the wheels to minimize wheel-spin and maximize traction. This is usually done by matching the speed of the rear wheels to that of the front wheels

White flag

A white flag warns drivers of a slow moving vehicle on the track

Wing or aerofoil

A type of upside-down, wing-shaped fixture that provides maximum downforce used to keep the car firmly on the track at high speed

Yellow flag

A yellow flag indicates danger such as a stranded car or an accident ahead

Notes on Sources

Web-based

CNN Sports. www.sportsillustrated.cnn.com

Motorsport.com. www.motorsport.com

Sports Illustrated www.si.com

The Formula One Database. www.f1db.com/tiki-index.php

The Official Formula One Website. www.formula1.com

Canadian Racer. www.motorsportscentral.com

F1-Live.com www.f1.racing-live.com

Pitpass.com www.pitpass.com

Racing Press www.racingpress.com

Universal Auto www.universalauto.com

Autosport 50th Anniversary Edition, July 13 2000
www.autosport.com

The Cahier Archive www.f1-photo.com

Vintage Race Car Journal www.vintageracecar.com

Instituto Ayrton Senna www.senna.globo.com (Brazil)

Ferrari World (Official Ferrari website)
www.ferrariworld.com/FWorld

Books

Hillier, V.A.W. *Hillier's Fundamentals of Motor Vehicle Technology.* 4th
    Edition. Cheltenham: Nelson Thornes Ltd,1991.

Legate Trevor. *100 Years Of Grand Prix: Celebrating A Century Of Grand
    Prix Racing 1906-2006* Kent: Touchstone Books Ltd, 2006.

Ecclestone, Bernie. *The Official Formula One Seaon Review 2005.* Som-
    erset: Haynes Publishing, 2005.

Jones, Bruce. *The Complete Encyclopedia of Formula One.* Dubai: Carl-
    ton Books, 2002.

Vergeer, Koen *Formula One Fanatic.* London: Bloomsbury, 2004

Glenda Fordham

Born in England, raised in the wilds of Western
Australia, Glenda Fordham continues to lead an
exciting life. She's been a comedy club manager,
a celebrity minder, tour manager and producer,
working with stars like Jim Carrey, Billy Crystal, Jay
Leno, Reba McEntire and Vince Gill. But in the last
10 years, she's found a consuming passion for the
fast life—car racing. She spends her Saturdays and
her summers glued to the TV watching races and
comparing stats on the drivers and their crews. She
loves the thrill of the race, the powerful cars, the skill
of the drivers—and especially the stories behind it
all. Glenda has written two other books on racing—
Greatest Stock Car Races and *Hottest Stock Car Drivers*.